(3) Ten kilos of Heroin seized in Guadalajara, Mexico

(4) Costa Rica makes Sedillo a member of its Narcotics Unit

MA COUNTRY ATTACHE ART SEDILLO (RED
LT. JORGE "LENO" LATINEZ AT CRASH SITE
AT A BANANA FINCA OUTSIDE DAVID, PANAMA

(5) With Lino and others during $2,000,000 cocaine seizure

To Steve & Judy

Hope you enjoy

Arthur M. Sedillo

CPSIA information can be obtained
at www.ICGtesting.com
Printed in the USA
BVHW08s1138250618
519964BV00006B/695/P

9 781478 797470

Don't Expect Anything

ARTHUR M. SEDILLO

outskirts
press

Outskirts Press, Inc.
http://www.outskirtspress.com

ISBN: 978-1-4787-9747-0

Outskirts Press and the "OP" logo are trademarks belonging to Outskirts Press, Inc.

PRINTED IN THE UNITED STATES OF AMERICA

TABLE OF CONTENTS

CHAPTER 1

MY FIRST ENCOUNTER with a policeman was a few days after I was born on February 2, 1938, in West Las Vegas, New Mexico. My godfather, Sheriff Frank Burged, held me in his arms as I was baptized Arthur Marcello Sedillo at Our Lady of Sorrows Church.

I was six years when I ran into a policeman a second time. It was summer, and usually on weekends, Mom would take my sisters Agnes and Judy and me to either the West Las Vegas Plaza Park or the East Las Vegas Lincoln Park.

On one of these Saturdays I patiently waited for us to go on our stroll, but no one else was getting on with the program; therefore, I took off on my own to the Plaza Park, even though I had only a vague idea of its location.

When I arrived at the park, I played on the ill-maintained lawn and then sat on a bench. At that moment realized I didn't have the slightest idea how to get back home. I started crying until a policeman walked up to me and asked, "What's the problem, kid?" I told him, "I'm lost." As he walked me to the nearby police station on Bridge Street, he said, "Don't worry; I'll telephone your parents to come for you." I thought that would be a neat trick, since we didn't have a telephone.

Inside the police station, the officer gave me a lollipop and told me to sit on a chair behind the counter. I sat and enjoyed my candy, ignoring the chitchat among the police officers and visiting public until I heard a familiar male voice say, "How can a parent be so careless losing their child at the park?"

I walked around the counter and said, "Daddy!"

Dad had been next door getting a haircut and had just popped in to visit his police friends. It took him a long time to live down this joyful humiliation. As he took me home piggyback, he told me how thankful he was that the policeman had found me. I told him, "When I grow up, I will become a policeman."

Dad went along with my life prediction but cautioned me not to take off alone, pointing out potential dangers. We stopped at Ludi's grocery store, and he bought me an ice cream cone, knowing that a spanking was forthcoming from Mom; however, he was able to soften her up a bit for me, resulting only in some corner time-out.

During these preadolescent years, I developed the ability to piss off my contemporaries as well as those older than me. My paternal grandmother, Carlota Gold de Sedillo, aka Mamatita, always came to my rescue She contributed to my misbehavior in the sense that I copied her foul mouth, which got me into more trouble.

Because of my poor physical condition and foul mouth, I became the neighborhood punching bag. To reduce ass kickings, I developed defense mechanisms that were more theatrical than practical. For example, when I was beaten up I faked fainting. I copied this ploy from a kid who suffered epileptic seizures. Unfortunately my dead possum role was not believable, because of my limited acting abilities.

Being more realistic, I started carrying a small notebook that snugly fit in the rear of my Levi trouser pocket. Each time someone beat me up, I would take it out and jot down the bully's name under the title Revenge List. Right then and there I vowed that when I grew up and became stronger, I would track down those bullies and beat them.

My hometown, West Las Vegas, rests on the saltpeter grasslands east of the Sangre to Cristo Mountain range about eighty miles east of our state capital, Santa Fe, New Mexico. The Gallinas (Chicken) River, which is merely a struggling creek, serves as the political division between West and East Las Vegas. This division, like the Rio Grande that separates the United States from Mexico, also divides the ethnic populations. Mostly affluent Anglos and shit kickers reside on the east side, while we primarily middle-class and poor Hispanics live on the west side. Our generation humorously referred to this river-political division as the Tortilla Curtain.

My parents, Phil G. Sedillo and Lucy Martinez Sedillo, came from distinct social backgrounds. My paternal grandparents had fifteen kids and were dirt poor. Ten had died before I was born. The remaining had dropped out of school to help maintain the family.

Mom's parents were more affluent and educated. Her father, Jose Martinez, was the West Las Vegas School superintendent. My maternal grandmother, more than just a housewife, ran a small grocery store next to their residence on Moreno Street.

I was born in that store after it was converted into a one-room apartment. Mom told me that President Abraham Lincoln was born in a one-room cabin also. Even at that young age, I knew Mom was setting a goal for me that was beyond my reach.

During World War II, Dad was declared a medical 4-F because of a back injury, disqualifying him from joining the military; therefore, his contribution to the war effort was relocating to San Diego, California, to work as a battleship painter.

The rest of our family remained in West Las Vegas, residing right across from the Sedillo clan. Grandma Mamatita and her two sons Zacharias and Cruz and their families lived on the east side of the 800 block of Chavez Street.

In the summer of 1944, Mom, my sisters, and I rode the train to visit Dad in California. That day-long train ride was a highlight of my youth, even though I caused Mom some difficult moments.

I met and befriended a black boy about my age who was traveling with his parents. His father was the train porter. I played awhile with my new friend, and then I excused myself and went to the bathroom and returned with a soapy washcloth and tried to wipe the black off my new friend's face. Even though both mothers laughed at my innocence, Mom was embarrassed and apologized to the kid's mother that this was the first time I had encountered a black person.

I behaved for the remainder of the trip except for an incident that has caused me lifelong stress. While eating in the dining car, I discreetly peeled an orange and placed the seeds in my shirt pocket. That night after the overhead lights were turned off, I faked falling into the aisle. When I got up, I told Mom that most of my teeth had fallen off. I opened my hand and showed her the orange seeds, telling her they were my teeth. Mom panicked and called the porter, who quickly came and shined his bright flashlight on my hand. I burst out laughing when they identified the orange seeds. I received a deserved spanking.

As a result of this incident, I have recurring nightmares that my teeth are coming loose and falling out. I have to keep removing the loose teeth immediately, because newer ones keep growing and pushing the older ones out. It reminds me of how sharks shed their assembly-belt-type teeth. In my dream I start getting tired and know that at a certain point I will no longer be able to take out my accumulating loose teeth and I will suffocate and die. I wake up in a cold sweat, convinced that these nightmares must be God's humorous way of punishing me for scaring Mom.

After the war, Dad and Mom saved enough money to buy a lot on Independence Street and construct our first house. Our new home was half a block from the political Gallinas River division. Our paved street also served as Highway 85. These two factors, a paved street and residing close to Gringolandia, upgraded our social status. The highlight of the housewarming party was Dad flushing the interior toilet for his amusement and envy of friends and relatives. I would somewhat miss the traditional two- and three-seater outhouses where my cousins and I took dumps together, talked, and checked out the Montgomery Ward department store catalog. We would crumple and use the last, softer, yellow pages as toilet paper.

My formal education started at Our Lady of Sorrows Parochial Elementary School. Since we didn't have a car, Mom had to get up early to fix us breakfast and get us ready to walk the half mile to school. From there she continued another half mile to her teaching job at North Public Elementary School.

On extremely cold mornings I mastered a technique prolonging a burp, giving the impression that I had an attack of acid indigestion. To further my scam, I faked vomiting my earlier consumed coffee with milk.

Mom probably knew I was pulling some shit, but if it was an extremely cold morning, she would let me stay with our dear neighbors, the Auntunas. Their small and cozy house was always warm with both heat and affection.

My parochial education came to a screeching halt in the second grade. Mom accompanied me to the inquisition-like conference with Sisters Martina and Manuela. The M&M nuns itemized my litany of sins, highlighting what had taken place the previous afternoon.

A girl classmate who sat on the desk in front of me was always turning around and teasing me without drawing attention to herself. Unfortunately each time I reacted to her bullshit, Sister Manuela, who had her back to us explaining something on the blackboard, turned around and caught me hitting or giving the finger to my provocateur.

Of course each time I was caught, the classmate has nothing but a fake angelic expression, playing the role of the blameless victim.

During the previous day's last period, I made up my mind to get even with this troublemaker. With stealth and dexterity I carefully untied the bow in the back of her pink dress. I fastened each strap end to the metal brackets of her seat, knowing that when the bell rang, she would jump straight up and run to the door. I knew that when she jumped up her straps would snap her right back to her seat, and I would have the last laugh, or so I thought.

Unfortunately for me, when the bell rang, she jumped up and dashed toward the door, when she must have felt a draft on her rear end, because the rear of her dress had torn off and remained attached to the desk. She covered her back with one hand, cried, and pointed at me with her other hand, accusing me of the misdeed.

After itemizing all my evil deeds to Mom, Sister Manuela demanded an explanation for my behavior. Pleading guilty to my last incident, I unnecessarily added, "When Saint Joseph and our Blessed Virgin Mother took Jesus to the House of David, Jesus got lost for three days at the temple, and he was twelve years old. I'm only eight, so what's the big deal?"

That did it. My misquotation of scripture blew the nuns' fuses, and I quickly hid behind Mom as she told them that my parochial education was over.

On the following Sunday Mass, as usual, I sat next to Mom's cousin's old-maid teachers Charlotte and Francis Martinez on their personal pew. They heard about my expulsion, and they too kicked me out of their seat. Charlotte pointed across the aisle and told me, "From now on, you sit across the aisle, right under the statue of Saint Jude, the saint of impossible causes. Maybe he can help you." My new seating location was indeed a blessing. Saint Jude became my patron saint.

The following school year, I had to walk a mile accompanying Mom to the North Public School where she enrolled me in the third grade. I would have preferred attending the South Public School, which was a lot closer to home, and most of my relatives and friends attended it.

The only negative thing about this relocation was that being the son of a teacher was a built-in motive to get my ass kicked continually by dumbasses. On the positive side, I enjoyed my midmorning snack and picnic-like lunches at noon with Mom in her classroom. Because of these meals and long walks to and from school, my health improved.

At the end of that school year, Mom agreed that my health was more in jeopardy from getting my ass kicked by the dumbasses; therefore she

DON'T EXPECT ANYTHING

decided that I finish my elementary education at South Public School.

My health continued improving, but my social traits didn't. As a rule I spent the majority of the time alone by choice.

As soon as the school year ended, my summer schedule changed significantly. I slept later and woke up to the sweet scent of the lilac bushes blooming right outside my open screened window. The sound of the chirping birds reminded me that a beautiful day awaited me.

Once I had breakfast and took care of my minor chores, it was free time for the rest of the day. Usually I accompanied Mom, walking toward the Gallinas River. At the Independence Bridge, I would exit left to the Gallinas Creek, while Mom continued to Highlands University to finish her post-graduate studies.

I fished with my homemade rod for trout that rarely made it downstream from the Montezuma Dam located five miles upstream. My usual catch was the ugly suckers, which I would drop on the creek side for hawks and other small mammals to devour.

When I reached the wooded area directly behind the Saint John Baptist De La Salle Christian Brother's seminary, I would hunt for chipmunks and squirrels with my bow and rubber-tipped arrows. When I hit one of these critters, the arrow would bounce off, scaring them shitless but leaving them unharmed. However, if I saw a snake, I would whip out my slingshot and kill it. This was done in retribution for the devil converting himself into a snake and tempting Eve to eat the fruit of the forbidden tree.

At noon I would return home for lunch and then walk back to the same wooded area, but for a different purpose. I would sneak into the La Salle Brothers seminary, disregarding the No Trespassing signs on the fence.

The seminary campus included several acres of athletic fields, gardens, and orchards. A formidable U-shaped two-story building was on the west side of the campus. Behind the building was a twenty-five foot rock grotto with a statue of Our Blessed Virgin Mary commemorating her appearance at Lourdes, France.

Before sneaking into the campus, I would spy on the brothers who were playing baseball. When they finally went inside and I could hear their Gregorian chant that was my signal to sneak further into the campus toward the grotto.

At the grotto, I would kneel and pray to our Blessed Virgin Mary and to Saint Jude to make me stronger so I could beat up the guys listed in my little notebook.

One day after my pious pit stop, I ran around the seminary building and jumped the rock-channeled ditch to Gonzales Street. I saw an older guy from the neighborhood. He was wearing a pink shirt, and I asked him if he had borrowed it from his sister. This comment earned me another ass kicking.

To prevent explaining to my parents my bloody nose and shirt, I detoured to Mamatita's house. I knew Grandma would wash my shirt and cover up for me. As I sat shirtless on top of Grandma's chopped wood pile, I sulked and my faith started to dwindle. I thought, "How can I just finish praying a whole rosary to become physically stronger, and shortly after, what happens? I get my ass kicked again."

As I toiled with these negative thoughts, Tio Joe Kavanagh came out of his elderly parents' house next door and walked to the wooden fence separating the properties. He was a distant uncle, but all of us, Mamatita's grandkids, called him Tio (uncle) as an endearment. Grandma helped raise him.

Tio Joe told me, "I bet that you are in trouble again. You know that Tuddy (his younger brother) and I have noticed that you keep pissing off all the guys in the neighborhood, right?"

I was not about to lie to him. Not only did we all love and respect him, but he was also the West Las Vegas police chief. As I started to explain my predicament, he patted me on the head and told me, "Tuddy and I have decided to teach you how to defend yourself, but you have to promise us to fight back only when you are defending yourself. Will you agree to do that?"

"Yes, Tio Joe. You will not believe it, but I have even been praying to learn how to defend myself."

He said, "Sure you are," knowing I wasn't the most pious kid on the block.

Tio Joe jumped the fence and joined me as we walked into Mama Tita's kitchen. She invited us to have coffee and some freshly baked sweet bread. Tio Joe told her, "Hold back on the goodies for a while, Grandma. Art and I are going to be busy for a while in your living room."

Grandma's house had only two rooms, the kitchen/dining room, and the living/bedroom. In the bedroom, she had an antique bureau with a large circular mirror that we were going to use for my first shadow boxing lesson.

Tio Joe instructed me, "I want you to stand up straight and then take a step forward with your left foot. Place both your arms close to your body, then extend your left hand a bit." As he spoke, he demonstrated what he wanted me to do as we both saw our reflection in the mirror.

"Now you will shoot your left hand straight out, and as you are doing it, turn your wrist to the right. If you don't, you could sprain or even break your wrist when you hit your opponent. This punch is called a left jab."

He then taught me how to throw a right cross, left hook, and uppercuts. He also taught me how to move my feet as I was throwing those punches. After he drilled me for about fifteen minutes, Grandma popped in, telling us the bread was getting cold.

Tio Joe told her, "Grandma, we will be right there, but you will not believe it. Art is a natural boxer. He has picked up all my instructions correctly."

After finishing the drill, I glanced at Grandma's statue of the Blessed Virgin Mary, and I could have sworn that she smiled, letting me know that my prayers were not in vain.

Tio Joe told me that he and Tuddy would be giving me additional boxing lessons but requested that besides Grandma and my parents, I should keep this training a secret. I promised as I hugged him for coming to my aid.

Both Tio Joe and Tuddy continued giving me serious boxing lessons in their converted garage gym, where I learned to hit the light speed bag and the heavy bag. Both Kavanagh brothers had excelled in their military service boxing tournaments.

CHAPTER 2

CARLOS GALLEGOS, MY childhood best friend, also lived across the street from the Sedillo clan on Chavez Street. We both struggled during these preteen years, continually pissing off our neighborhood peers and others.

We visited the East Las Vegas Tilden Park on summer Sunday evenings for the sole purpose of protecting the virginity of some local teenage girls we didn't even know. These girls would go to the park to make out with the Air Force personnel stationed at Camp Luna.

We played the role that we were knights or crusaders with the moral obligation to protect the honor of these flyboy groupies. We would sneak up on the couples and try to scare them by yelling, just about the time when they were about to perform the dirty deed. Once we shook them up, we ran like hell out of the park laughing our asses off, usually spoiling the couples' romantic interludes.

On one of these Sunday nights, we almost got caught, so we decided on getting additional reinforcements. On the following Sunday night, we talked Joe "Lile" Griego to accompany us. Lile was a couple of years older than us and built like a bull. We knew that with him, we would be able to better defend ourselves in the event the flyboys caught us.

He was reluctant to join us but eventually agreed. When we reached the park, it was starting to get dark, and the few park pole lights were turned on. As we approached the couples, we noticed them already in a romantic mood at the mid-park gazebo bandstand. We instructed Lile to get down flat on the ground like us and crawl toward our target just how we had seen actor John Wayne play the role of a U.S. Marine in the war movie *Sands of Iwo Jima*.

The night was quiet for the exception of crickets chirping and the girls giggling. All of a sudden at about halfway to our destination, we heard sirens and saw two police units beaming their spotlights at us from opposite sides of the park.

We jumped up and ran like hell out of the park and around the block to an alley behind Tilden Street. At the center of the alley, a wooden fence curved at a forty-five-degree angle on both sides of a garage. Carlos jumped on top of the garage and hid there. I saw a homemade cement mixer resembling a small boat resting upside down on the ground. I lifted it and hid under it.

We hid as the police entered the alley from both directions. Lile, who was a bit clumsy not able to hide, kept yelling, "What should I do? What should I do?"

Neither Carlos nor I said a damn thing, hoping he would shut the hell up and hide. Instead he just stood there. A moment later the police were at the scene and grabbed his ass. Instead of playing it cool, he lifted the cement mixer with his free hand and told me, "Art, get up. They caught us." I was lying in a fetal position in total disbelief that Lile had exposed my hideout. Carlos, seeing what took place, started laughing. The police heard him and dragged his ass down.

At the station the police chewed our asses out. We were afraid of being thrown in jail, but after we explained our crusader role that we were attempting to save the ladies of the village from being deflowered, the police were a bit amused but didn't believe our bullshit, accusing us of being juvenile voyeurs.

The officer in charge said, "Those girls' conduct is none of your damn business, and you stupid kids should be thankful that those servicemen reported you instead of kicking your asses. Now get the hell out of here, and we'd better not see you at that park again. Do you understand?"

We all acknowledged with a happy "Yes, sir!" After we exited the building, we could hear the police laughing about how Lile had exposed us from our hiding place. Carlos and I smiled but didn't say shit, knowing Lile would kick our asses.

Once we reached our home turf, Lile turned around and pointed his shaking finger at us stating, "Don't you dare ever, ever invite me to go anyplace with you guys, okay?"

The police impressed me with how they handled this incident. They admonished us and scared the hell out of us, but they released us without documenting our detention. I knew I would have to clean up my act if I ever wanted to fulfill my aspirations of becoming a policeman.

Sometimes one can get into trouble even without initiating the problem. Again Carlos and I experienced an adverse incident during our preteen years.

During the summer months we would hike to a waterhole we called La Guitarra. We named it this because the rock formation surrounding the swimming hole resembled a guitar. When we walked the two miles to La Guitarra, we always carried an empty gunnysack so we could pick *quelites* (wild spinach) on our way back. We didn't like it, but our parents did.

On one of these trips, we saw a large batch of *quelites* growing inside a fenced area. We crossed there, and in no time we almost filled our sack. As we started walking back to the dirt road, we noticed a teenage Anglo guy riding a beautiful albino horse toward us. At first we thought he was waving at us in a friendly manner; however, as he approached us, we noticed he had a bullwhip, and he started hitting us with it as he hollered at us, "Get the fuck out of my land, you dirty Mexicans!"

Carlos and I panicked but had sense enough to run toward the fence at different angles to get fewer whippings. Unfortunately the well-trained horse pranced from one of us to the other. We finally got to the fence and jumped to safety as the shit-kicker picked up our gunny sack and emptied its contents.

As he galloped away we yelled at him that we were Spanish-American and probably cleaner than him.

After this horrible experience, I studied the shit-kickers physical profile and logged him in my revenge notebook, identifying him as "horse face."

As I struggled and terminated my sixth-grade education at South Public School, our West Las Vegas community was blessed with what we considered a miracle.

The Saint John Baptist de La Salle Christian Brothers decided to relocate their seminary to their established Saint Michael's College at Santa Fe. They sold their campus to the West Las Vegas School system, and part of the sale contract included a stipulation that some of the Christian Brothers would remain in town for a while to assist in converting the campus into West Las Vegas's own middle and high school.

Brother Bernard became the high school principal, and Brothers Abel, Nicholas, and Luke assisted in teaching and athletics. Some of the local teachers, including Mom, were transferred to our high school.

The former North and South Public Elementary rivals would join forces and become a formable athletic team. "Go gold and green Dons!"

My seventh-grade teacher, Brother Able, was in his early thirties, had blond hair and blue eyes, and was in top physical condition. His no-nonsense and pious attitude quickly earned him the respect and admiration of all the school staff and student body. His athletic abilities, especially in football, were outstanding. He could barefoot kick the football almost the length of the football field. It was said that the NFL would have easily drafted him.

During the football team's daily practice I sat on the sidelines observing and enjoying the Don's scrimmages. Once the training was over, and all vacated the area I would sneak over to the Blessed Virgin Mary grotto, and like in my younger years, pray for my continued improved health.

The following year, Mom became my eighth-grade teacher, and I could not afford to embarrass her by screwing up, so I had to intensify my study habits. At my eighth-grade graduation I had the satisfaction that even though I was not the top academic student, I was close to it. I teased Mom that I intentionally dropped my high-grade scores so that the other kids would not think that she had improved my grades to make me look smarter.

Upon graduating, I hoped to qualify for the varsity football team the following school year. As I walked up to the school stage to pick up my eighth-grade diploma, I observed Brother Abel having what appeared to be an intense conversation with Mom.

Later at home, I asked Mom about her talk with Brother Abel. She asked all us family members to listen to what she had to say. She said, "Brother Able told me that he and the other brothers are convinced that God has blessed our family with a vocation that since two to three years before the high school was formed, they had observed you sneaking into the seminary campus and praying at the grotto. The brothers feel you have a vocation to become a Christian brother and should consider going to their seminary in Lafayette, Louisiana."

I was in shock but failed to explain that the reason I was praying all that time was to become healthy so I could kick the shit out of the bullies beating me up. I concluded that it must be payback time for my prayers being answered, and now I would have to join God's team. The following autumn I was on a Greyhound bus on my way to the Saint John Baptist De La Salle Seminary in Lafayette, Louisiana.

My transformation from a quasi-juvenile delinquent to a seminarian would need something close to a miracle, so without a doubt I would have to clean up my act. Not only would I have to forget about becoming a policeman, but now that my puberty hormones were starting to kick in, I would also have to renounce any flirtatious contact with girls.

Arriving in Louisiana was a shocking experience. The warm, humid weather and vegetation all over the place, including Spanish moss hanging from trees, certainly made me feel like I had entered a strange wonderland.

The seminary grounds were located in a beautiful campus that included several brick buildings surrounded by nicely manicured lawns and several orchards, including pecan, pear, and apple trees. The main building housed the classrooms and dormitory. The second structure included the kitchen/dining area. It also contained the chapel and the novitiate seminarian's quarters.

I quickly learned that this institution was going to be something like a Christian boot camp. At the break of dawn, one of the brothers entered the dormitory and clapped his hands as the signal for all of us seminarians to get up, roll out of bed, quickly make our beds, and then kneel and say our morning prayers. After a quick shower, we cleaned up the dormitory, halls, bathrooms, and classrooms.

At seven in the morning we attended Mass, followed by breakfast. After breakfast we finished other cleaning duties, including the gym and swimming pool area. On Saturdays we all worked maintaining the campus lawn, orchards, and vegetable gardens.

Classes started at nine and lasted until five in the afternoon with a lunch break. Since the Christian Brothers founder Saint John Baptist de La Salle was French, learning that language was compulsory.

My favorite school activity was the physical education, in which we would play the sport in season. After working out in the athletic field, we would freshen up with a swim in the pool, have supper, and sing vespers in the chapel.

Between vespers and homeroom study, we were allowed a short period to write home or just have a general free period. By nine we hit the sack, and the same routine was repeated daily.

During the athletic program, all games were in-house with surrounding De La Salle High School teams that would come and play with us on our campus. These games were recognized as only practice games for the visiting varsity teams, since we were not included in standard high school athletics programs. Of course female cheerleaders and the general public were excluded from our games.

On one of these practice games, the offensive team got frustrated with my constant tackling its quarterback, so they all jumped on me. My right arm was disjointed at the elbow, and I was rushed to the hospital.

While I was at the hospital, retired Brother Jerome accompanied me during my three-day stay. After I was released with a full arm cast, Brother Jerome escorted me to the doctor's office for follow-up therapy. He told me, "Arturo, the coach of the team that broke your arm said that he would do anything to have you on his team."

I don't know why, but I got the feeling that Brother Jerome was indirectly telling me that I should consider returning home to play varsity sports in high school and college.

On Wednesday evenings our study period was shorter because of an Advertisement of Defects session. All the students entered the large study hall, sat, and waited for their turn to walk up in front of Brother Director Daniel's elevated desk. Dressed in his black robe and with his stern disposition, he had the appearance of a judge conducting judicial duties.

He would tap his silver-plated pen on his desk, which was the signal for the next student to walk to the designated location in front of his desk.

Once this was done, any Juniorate could stand up and give some charitable criticism to the upfront guy. As a rule, each student received at least three admonishments, ranging from keeping dirty, sweaty socks in the closet to chewing with the mouth open, and so forth.

On one of these sessions, one of the students criticized me. "My brother Arthur, you tend to defraud your fellow brothers by trickery and deceit."

Hearing this, Brother Director demanded my accuser to clarify his remark further.

Referring to the gift exchange policy in which only holy cards are authorized as currency to barter in exchange for gifts sent from home, my accuser explained that I had defrauded him by using phony holy cards.

We earned holy cards through good merits, including good grades and related activities.

My accuser came from a wealthy family that regularly mailed him real nice goodies. He was asking for a hundred holy cards in exchange for his red Swiss Army knife. I wanted that knife but only had ten holy cards. I went to the supply room, and using a paper cutter and a hole puncher, I cut ninety cards to the same dimensions as the ten real holy cards and punched several holes through them so they could be "holey."

I sandwiched the homemade ninety cards between the ten real holy cards, five on top and five on the bottom of the stack, and quickly flashed them to the guy as I negotiated for his knife. "Here are the hundred cards that you want."

He handed me his knife and then threw a tantrum, telling me that I had cheated him. I told him I had not. "I gave you a hundred cards of which ninety have holes in them, and the other ten are regular holy cards. I also splashed holy water on them, therefore making them 'holy.'"

When my accuser finished explaining how I had defrauded him, I could have sworn that I saw Brother Director almost crack a smile, but he quickly regained his usual stern composure and admonished me to return the knife to my accuser.

At the end of July all of us seminarians were in a joyous mood. On August first, we got our summer break and were allowed to go home for one month. Before departing, we had a one-on-one conference with Brother Director.

During my session I sat in front of the director's desk as instructed.

He turned around and started playing his reel-to-reel recorder and asked me, "I want you to listen to the sound, and want you to identify it, okay?"

"Yes, Brother Director."

I immediately recognized the snare-drum roll sound and told him, "That's the sound of a punching bag banging the platform."

"That is correct, and can you tell me who is hitting the bag?"

"Brother Director, it had to be me. When I broke my arm, the doctor instructed me to exercise both arms as much as possible. Brother Jerome helped me set up the speed bag under the basement staircase. My parents mailed it to me."

Brother Director continued. "Do you realize that at the time you were hitting your bag, you were supposed to be quietly walking around the campus meditating and saying your rosary?"

"Yes, Brother Director, I was meditating in my own way. As I punched the bag, I was imagining that I was punching the heck out of the devil."

For the first time, I heard Brother Director laugh. He laughed so much that tears came out of his eyes. He stood up, wiped his eyes, gave me a fatherly hug, and stated, "My dear son, I must tell you that our Lord has some special mission for you out there in this troubled world. Go in peace."

When I walked out of his office, another brother was more informal and told me to pack all my belongings because I would not be returning to the seminary.

After the news settled in, I went through a series of mixed feelings. The seminary life had intensified my spirituality, and I thoroughly enjoyed it, but at times I wondered if I was worthy of such a vocation.

When I boarded the school bus that took several of us to the Greyhound Bus Depot, I felt better, realizing that I was not the only one who had been canned. Several others also had a one-way ticket.

At the age of fourteen years I was on my way back home, and during that long bus ride, I had several hours to reflect on what might be in store me for the rest of my life. As I evaluated what had transpired during the previous year, I concluded that even though I had not been blessed with a religious vocation, I would forever be grateful for having the opportunity of coexisting with so many pious and honorable people. If nothing else, I hoped and prayed that some of these qualities might have rubbed off on me.

I was also grateful that my physical fitness had significantly improved, and I looked forward to joining our hometown football team. As I dozed off with the assistance of the soothing sound of the bus rolling along, I visualized the cheerleaders and other girls cheering my athletic efforts.

CHAPTER 3

MY ARRIVAL AT home was a joyous, tear-jerking, family reunion. Once the hugs and tears were over, I explained, "I want you to know that I answered God's call to see if I was blessed with a calling, but after a year's try, I learned that God has other plans for me in this troubled world. Now I have to continue my education and prayers, and in due time my life's goal will surface."

I settled into a comfortable groove and eagerly waited for the school year to start so I could join the West Las Vegas High School football team.

It would never happen. Our high school was temporarily shut down because of some state accreditation requirement, a shock to the West Las Vegas community. Only the junior high school survived.

The West Side High School students that were able to continue their education had two options. They could attend their rival East Las Vegas High or attend the East Las Vegas private Catholic Immaculate Conception (IC) High School.

Since my parents had struggled financially to send me to the seminary, there was no way I was going to burden them with the additional expense of attending IC High School.

I would attend East Las Vegas Public High School. After resolving my school problems, getting a job during the remainder of the summer became my priority. Dad was by then employed by the Highland University maintenance crew as a painter. On weekends he would moonlight painting houses in the affluent east side area. He got me a job at one of his clients at a beautiful ranch-type house on the seventh street extension. My job involved mowing the large lawn and weeding the flower beds surrounding the house. At the seminary I had learned about gardening, so I felt confident in my job assignment. At the end of the hard-worked day, the owner was satisfied and referred me to several other clients.

Toward the end of the summer vacation, football fever was in the air. What the hell, my favorite gold and green Dons no longer existed, so playing with their rival red and white Cardinals would not make me disloyal. I reported to the Vegas High football field two weeks before the school year started.

Most of the varsity players appeared to be on hand. The coach directed them to regular conditioning and scrimmaging activities. He assigned his assistant coach to a group of us rookies. The assistant coach processed us through several activities.

I caught all the passes thrown to me, and I threw passes farther than anyone else. I also kicked the ball farther than the other aspirants. The following day I was instructed to report to the head coach's office. I felt confident that as a result of my accomplishments on the previous day I would be assigned to the regular varsity squad.

The head coach told me, "Art, you just don't know how I would like to add you to our first-string team, but unfortunately I have some bad news. I have been informed that you come to us from an out-of-state school, and that makes you ineligible to participate in our varsity sports activities. I am very sorry, but there is nothing that I can do but comply with this regulation."

I said, "But Coach, how can that be? I only attended a Catholic seminary that did not have any organized varsity sports. We only practiced and scrimmaged with nearby Christian Brothers High Schools."

"I'm sorry, Art, like I told you. I don't make the rules. I will try to find out if we can make an exception in your case."

I never heard from him.

Sometime after, I learned that an eastside Chicano that had not performed as well in the rookie tryouts had tipped off the coach about my possible ineligibility.

This incident reminded me of advice my dad had given me about our Hispanic community. He told me, "Beware of our own *raza's* (race's) jealous nature. If a Chicano opens a grocery store, the Chicano neighbors will bypass it and travel a farther distance to the Safeway store, just to keep from giving the business to a fellow Chicano."

After school a few days later, I got off the school bus on South Pacific Street and strolled over to the old West Las Vegas High School grounds where only the junior high classes continued. I had heard that even though the Brothers had left, the statue of the Blessed Virgin Mary and grotto remained in the campus, so I went to check it out.

I was glad to see that the campus was empty as I approached the grotto, knelt down, and started praying. I had not finished my Hail Mary when I heard the sound of a punching bag coming from the nearby school basement.

I walked into the building hallway and on down to the nearby basement. Several familiar guys were working out in what had been converted into a makeshift boxing gym. They were training in preparation to participate in the AAU Golden Gloves Boxing Tournament.

I pleasantly thought about the coincidence that the same sound of the speed bag that caused me to be shit canned out of the seminary had directed me from the grotto to a boxing gym. I had no doubts that this heavenly omen had a message for me to become a boxer or some kind of fighter.

I recognized Mr. Timmy Solano. He had been my history teacher in junior high, and he was one of the West Las Vegas High School assistant football coaches. He introduced me to boxing coach Mr. Junio Lopez, an auto parts salesman.

I was accepted into the Golden Gloves training team. To get into good physical condition, instead of taking the school bus out of East High School, I started running back to the West Las Vegas gym every afternoon.

After working out a couple of weeks, we were kicked out of the basement. The school principal informed our trainers that the school insurance could not cover a non-school sporting activity.

Coach Junio Lopez talked to the Immaculate Conception High School nuns, who approved that we continue working out in their school basement, providing the school would not be liable for any related injuries. This relocation, as far as I was concerned, was another omen directing me to become a fighter.

Our team's first tournament was in the northern village of Chama. When we got there, we found out that the local bar/dance hall had been converted into a boxing arena for the event. Several surrounding communities sent their teams.

All our team members were excited but admitted feeling butter-flies, this being our first boxing match. Unfortunately the only other lightweight (135 pounds) boxer was my teammate Robert Maez, so we had to box each other. Robert was a real nice guy and enjoyed a muscular build. The only thing that I had going for me was speed, and I was able to hit and run out of my opponent's punches. I won the fight on a unanimous decision and qualified for the regional tournament at Clovis, New Mexico.

The Regional Golden Gloves Boxing Tournament held at Clovis was much more urbane then the brawl we had at the Chama bar. I was matched with an Air Force guy on the first night and won a split decision. It was a tough fight, and it was my good conditioning that helped me win the fight, because in the third round my opponent petered out.

The following night I knocked out my opponent in the first round, and that performance spooked my subsequent opponent. Throughout the fight I kept chasing him all over the ring, earning me unanimous decisions and the regional championship.

Three weeks later I reported to the State Championship Tournament at the Roswell Military High School Academy.

I won my fights the first two nights, qualifying me for the state championship on the third and final tournament night. At the age of fifteen, I lost the state championship by a split decision.

That summer I boxed a couple of fights as an invited boxer with the Santa Fe boxing team. At Silver City, I knocked out a twenty-three-year-old ex-con in the first round. At Espanola, New Mexico, I won the fight against El Rito Boarding High School athletic star Lupe Juarez.

After the Espanola boxing event, the El Rito boxing team coach Jimmy Ortiz asked to talk to me. He was in his mid-forties with a slender build and walked with a small limp. His broken nose was the only clue to his being a former boxer.

He told me, "Look, Art, you are a talented fighter. How would you like to join our team? The El Rito Boarding School is only one of two state high schools that have a varsity boxing team. I'm almost sure that I may be able to get you a partial or maybe full athletic scholarship."

"Wow, that would be great, but about a year ago I burdened my parents by financing my freshman year at a seminary, and I surely can't tell them to pay for a boarding school. However, if you can get me a full scholarship, I would go for it."

Mr. Ortiz smiled and said, "The mere fact that you are an ex-seminarian, you are obviously a good kid, so I will really push hard to get you in. Just give me your parents' names and address so I can visit them if I can get the full scholarship."

"Okay." I gave him the information and told him I would be standing by to hear from him.

At the end of the summer, Mr. Ortiz came to Las Vegas and met with my parents, offering me a full paid boxing scholarship. On my insistence, they approved.

CHAPTER 3

El Rito, New Mexico, is located in the middle of nowhere approximately forty miles northwest from Espanola. When I got there, Mr. Ortiz registered me and then took me on a tour of the campus ending at the guys' dormitory, a sizeable pre-fab building. Besides being the boxing coach, he was a history teacher and our dormitory proctor.

When I went to supper at the mess hall, I noticed two Las Vegas students. Joan Burged, the daughter of my godfather, and Mary Lou. They both greeted me and asked me to join them at their table. Joan had already graduated from high school but was attending the cosmetology class. Mary Lou was a junior like me. I was happy to find these hometown students, and the three of us became very good friends. Mary Lou became my first girlfriend.

Coach Ortiz turned out to be an outstanding instructor, teacher, and role model. His boxing instructions were at times unorthodox, yet most positive. For example, he folded a newspaper into a cylinder shape and made me hold it between my right arm and the right side of my chest. He then instructed me to throw a right cross at the heavy bag. He would tell me, "I want you to punch the bag before the newspaper hits the floor."

This technique not only increased my punching speed but also, by lowering my head, it further reduced exposing it to my opponent's punches.

During the Albuquerque Golden Glove Regional Tournament, I won the novice class welterweight championship and went on to Roswell, New Mexico, where I won the state novice welterweight championship.

At the end of the school year, Principle Rodriguez told me, "Art, you piled a lot of credit hours while you were in the seminary. You need only three credit hours to graduate. If you join the military, we will gladly give you the additional three credit hours to complete your graduation without having to spend an additional year in high school."

I agreed with him and told him that I was planning to join the U.S. Marines.

CHAPTER 4

I WAS GLAD that in the summer of 1954 I sneaked into the New Mexico National Guard at the age of sixteen. With that basic military training, I felt more confident in joining the U.S. Marines.

In July 1955, I traveled on American Airlines from Albuquerque, New Mexico, to San Diego, California. Two fellow New Mexicans, Dennis Riley and David McDonald, accompanied me.

We arrived in San Diego at dusk, and the humidity smacked us as we deplaned on the wet tarmac. For a while we were disoriented but followed the other passengers through the thick fog into the terminal. We located the U.S. Marine waiting area and stood by it. Several other recruits from our and other flights joined us.

U.S. Marine Corporal Knutson approached us, and after counting us, instructed us to follow him to the parking lot. We boarded an olive green semi-bus that looked more like a cattle tractor-trailer than a human transporting vehicle.

Once inside the vehicle and with the door shut, Corporal Knutson went through a complete Dr. Jekyll-Mr. Hyde transformation from a nice guy to a stern bad-ass drill instructor as he yelled at us, "Okay, you bunch of shit birds, shut the fuck up. I will call out your names again, and you will respond. Do you understand?"

We acknowledged with "Yes, sir."

He chewed us out for referring to him as a sir. "I'm an enlisted U.S. Marine, and you will only address officers with the title of sir. Do you understand?"

We all responded with a simple "Yes."

The trip quickly ended as the bus traveled out of the airport terminal and circled to the adjacent property dodging in and out of traffic on the freeway. The entrance to Marine Corps Recruit Depot (MCRD) was through a rock archway with a large U.S. Marine emblem embossed on the center. Inside the base yellow stucco buildings with reddish tile roofs, Spanish hacienda-style, enclosed three sides of the square mile paved parade field.

The portal lights from the building arcades barely penetrated through the thick fog as we continued to the other end of the parade field to the receiving quarters. The forth side of the parade field has several Quonset huts that would be home for the next three months.

The bus stopped at the receiving building. Once it was dark and silent for a short while, we heard several repeated stomping noises coming from someplace within the foggy and wet parade field. Finally we noticed one of several marching recruit platoons. The noise we heard was of synchronized boot heels hitting the wet parade field. It was late at night, and those recruits were still out there marching in the fog and drizzling rain. It gave us a preview of what to expect.

The bus interior lights went on, and a thin bony-faced drill instructor sergeant popped into the bus and identified himself in a loud staccato voice. "My name is Sergeant D. D. Mielke, and I will be your chief drill instructor. Within the next three months at least a third of you, or maybe more, will be packaged and sent back to your mother's arms for additional nourishment because you are not fit to be U.S. Marines. The rest of you may make it, but don't count on it until graduation day. You will hate me, but I don't give a rat's ass. From here on out you will keep your damn traps shut and do what you are ordered, immediately. Now fall out into formation."

We complied, and after shuffling around in the dark finally stood in a somewhat acceptable formation. We were ordered to stand at attention. We remained in this position in complete darkness for more than an hour.

Finally Sergeant Mielke returned from the administrative building, stood in front of the formation, and yelled in a raspy voice, "Which of you shit birds can kick my ass?"

After a minute or so with no response, he added, "You will remain standing at attention until one of you shit for brains answers my question."

I shouted, "With all due respect, I think I can do it."

A short silence followed, and then Sergeant Mielke responded, "Front and center, shit bird."

I made a smart back step and marched around and in front of the sergeant, not knowing what to expect.

To my surprise, Sergeant Mielke yelled out to the troops, "Who can beat the shit out of this smart ass?"

Oh shit, I knew I had fucked up. This big Mexican named Perez from El Paso, Texas, said, "I can beat him." The guy had to be a heavyweight and tougher than a bull. I heard him talking at the airport, and I concluded that he was one dumb-ass loud mouthed son of a bitch, but now I realized that he probably would kick my ass. He was ordered to march front and center.

As he strolled toward me, I knew I would have to outwit the bull. I felt the water running down my face and didn't know if it was the light rain falling or if it was fear sweat. When Perez approached me, I kicked his balls, and he went down like a sack of shit. As I went to finish him up, both Sergeant Mielke and Corporal Kramer grabbed me and pulled me back.

Later I learned that this was the drill instructors' procedure in determining the selection of the platoon guide. Whatever their plan may have been, they must have modified their selection process after this incident, because both Perez and I were illuminated. A sharp-looking black guy named Herbert, who had college ROTC background, was designated as our guide. I got a runner-up position as one of four squad leaders. Perez didn't get shit.

The three months of boot camp were physically and psychologically excruciating, but my hometown buddies and I prevailed. One highlight incident came about during our battalion boxing smokers. These boxing smokers, in which boxers from the different platoons competed, were about the only entertainment we had.

When Sergeant Mielke asked for volunteers to fight in the smoker, he was not surprised when I raised my hand, and he cautioned me, "Okay, Sedillo, I'm going to let you fight, but remember, no kicking unless you want your ass kicked out of the Corps. Do you understand me?"

"Yes, Sergeant"

On fight night my proposed opponent became sick, and to my disappointment, my fight was canceled. However, the base varsity boxing coach, Tech/Sergeant Willie Moore who was conducting the boxing matches, said that his friend, a civilian professional boxer, was in the audience. He was my same weight, and if I would agree, we could have an exhibition bout in which the professional would hold back on his punches. As I agreed, I noticed a shitty smile on Sergeant Mielke's face. He was probably thinking that for sure I was going to get my ass kicked.

I saw the pro boxer sitting in the front ringside seats accompanied by two attractive black girls. When our bout was up, I distinctly heard him tell them, "I'll be right back. I'm going to go play with this kid."

When he jumped into the ring, he was wearing a flashy red and white robe and trunks and matching red boxing shoes. I was wearing the standard U.S. Marine boxer trunks, tennis shoes, and a white towel over my shoulders.

In the first round, my opponent came out throwing all kinds of jabs and doing some fancy footwork. Every once in a while he would side-step and wave at his girlfriends. After I slipped a couple of his punches and counter punched him, it was apparent that he got pissed, because contrary to our agreed exhibition rules, he started hitting me harder.

I responded in kind, and the roar of the audience was tremendous. After a flurry of punches, my opponent found himself on the floor completely knocked out. After the referee and medical corpsman attended and revived him, I walked by him and asked him, "Do you want to play some more?"

In October 1955, our platoon graduated with honors. I was one of five promoted to private first class. We were in formation for the last time as we stood by for our base assignments.

Sergeant Mielke called my name, "Private First Class Sedillo, front and center."

I marched for the last time in front of this man we all had learned to respect and admire. He continued, "You have the shortest assignment. Report to building twenty-nine, MCRD boxing varsity athletic section."

We shook hands and then he punched me on my PFC strips and wished me well. For the first time, he spoke to me as an equal, telling me that perhaps sometime we would meet at the NCO club and have a beer. That was the last time I saw him.

I picked up my duffle bag and walked the short distance to the MCRD Varsity Athletics Barracks. The boxing gym and administrative offices were on the ground floor and the dormitory on the second floor.

I walked through the mirror-clean, polished hall to Boxing Coach Moore's office. Tech/Sergeant Moore, a heavyset black guy in his mid-forties, greeted me in a friendly manner and said, "Okay, Sedillo, with the exception of saluting officers and once in a while doing guard duty, you can relax and forget boot camp. You are now a Marine. Welcome aboard."

He explained the workout schedule and other duties. "At two you will report to the gym for your regular workouts under my direction or one of my assistants. What you do after workouts and weekends is none of my business, as long as it is not against the U.S Military Code of Military Justice or laws of the land. Do you have any questions?"

"No, Sergeant Moore."

Sergeant Moore instructed administrative clerk Private Keyes to show me to my quarters after taking care of required administrative stuff. After explaining my duties, Private Keyes gave me a tour of the athletic barracks.

After I got my bunk and locker assignments and dropped off my duffle bag, Private Keyes walked with me to the first-floor boxing gym. The place was empty except for two boxers that were swabbing the floor and cleaning the area.

We went to dinner, and Private Keyes continued briefing me as we munched down on our chow. "You will see that the other base varsity teams, including football, basketball, and baseball players, will constantly be coming and going on their seasonal schedules. You boxers are the only year-round sport."

After a couple of weeks, Coach Sergeant Moore called me into his office and said. "Before we start going hard on our boxing schedule, I'm going to give you a break, and you can go on home leave for ten days."

I had limited funds, but Private Keyes came to my aid and lent me a hundred dollars. He also instructed me to get dressed in my uniform, and he dropped me off at the San Diego eastern city limits, telling me I would quickly get a ride hitchhiking.

He was right. Shortly after dropping me off, an old-time cowboy driving a pickup truck picked me up. He told me he was on his way to Flagstaff, Arizona. That was great and meant that from Flagstaff, I would be halfway home.

Unfortunately late that night he told me that he resided about twenty miles from Flagstaff and would be turning left to his ranch. He invited me to stay at his ranch and continue in the morning. I thanked him but told him my leave time was limited. He dropped me off and continued to his ranch.

Traffic was light and no one had told me that I would be freezing my ass in the Arizona desert nights. Finally after an hour and a half a black family driving a station wagon stopped and gave me a ride. The family was on the way to a funeral in Chicago. The driver's wife told me her husband had worked all day and been driving all this time and was dead tired. They were both glad when I relieved him and drove all the way to Albuquerque. From Albuquerque I took the Greyhound bus to my hometown.

My friends Carlos and Fernando were tipped off by Mom, and they were waiting for me at the bus depot.

They drove me home, and after a joyful reunion at home, I quickly changed into Levi's and a T-shirt and joined my friends and went to a dance at the Castaneda Hotel. I don't know what we were thinking, but going to a shit-kicking dance was setting us up for trouble.

Once inside, we noticed that we were the only Hispanics in the dance and obviously uninvited. Before hell broke loose, I saw the guy who had whipped Carlos and me with a bullwhip near the Guitarra waterhole several years before. I approached the guy and reminded him of the incident. He responded, "Get the hell out . . ." I didn't let him finish the sentence. I dropped him with a right cross to the jaw. Hell broke loose. All his buddies joined the fight, beating the hell out of us. Eventually we made it to the door and ran out of the place laughing our asses off.

I returned to San Diego MCRD Varsity Boxing Team and stayed at that post for an additional year and a half. We traveled all over the United States kicking ass most of the time.

While on my once-a-month weekend guard duty, I walked into the baseball players' dormitory, which should have been vacated the previous day. The lights were turned off, but I heard some guys laughing at the other end of the dormitory. I carefully sneaked closer to the group and noticed that they were smoking marijuana, I quickly backtracked and called the provost marshal's office.

CHAPTER 4

Shortly after three military police showed up, I led them to where the ballplayers were smoking marijuana. All five suspects were arrested and half a kilo of marijuana was confiscated.

The military police commander was most appreciative and suggested that I consider joining their outfit. Since I was not twenty-one years old yet, the required age to join the military police, I assured the commander that if I decided to ship over, I would consider such a transfer.

The commander enrolled me in a U.S. Marine correspondence criminal investigation training course. I studied the course and completed it. In doing so I had no doubt that once I finished my tour of duty, I would pursue my childhood dream to become a police officer.

A year later I was promoted to corporal and transferred to Twenty-nine Palms, a desert base near Palms Springs, California. At the new station I was assigned to the varsity boxing team under the direction of Tech/Sergeant Flores. That year I won the Southwestern United States Golden Gloves Championship at the Las Vegas, Nevada, Silver Slipper Casino and was awarded the outstanding boxer trophy for the tournament. (1)

Tech/Sergeant Flores, who was from the Los Angeles area, took me with him and introduced me to his family and friends, but most important, he took me to the famous Main Street Boxing Gym in downtown Los Angeles where he introduced me to professional boxing coach Baron Von Stumme. This coach assured me a position in his professional boxing stable when I finished my tour of duty.

At the end of my Twenty-nine Palms assignment, I was promoted to sergeant and transferred to the Camp Pendleton, California, U.S. Marine Boxing Team. After four years of service, I was honorably discharged and returned to New Mexico.

CHAPTER 5

THE TRANSITION FROM military to civilian life was smooth, since my privileged tour of duty as a "jock" and quick promotion to sergeant had significant advantages.

When I got home, most of my friends were married and couldn't come out and play. I was not ready to settle down. Instead I pursued my two priorities, going to college and becoming a policeman.

Enrolling at Highlands University was no problem, but I noticed that most of the other freshmen were four to five years younger than me. I befriended Andrew Salazar, who was more mature than the other average freshman.

My second priority was getting a job in the West Las Vegas Police Department, which would be more problematic because in my absence, our traditional Democratic West Las Vegas was now Republican. The only good thing going for me was that my former boxing coach, Junio Lopez, was the mayor.

I went to his auto parts store located in the Plaza Park. He greeted me with a macho hug telling me, "Art, thanks for your service to our country. I'm so proud of you. We have kept up with your continued success in boxing."

I congratulated him for being mayor and causing West Las Vegas to win the prestigious title of the U.S. All American City. After a few pleasantries, Mayor Lopez asked me, "What are your plans now, Art?"

"I'm glad you asked. I enrolled in Highlands University and plan to pursue a law enforcement career. While in the Marines I studied criminal justice. I was wondering if you had any vacancies in the police department."

He told me, "Art, before I answer, let me call George. I want him to listen to what you just said." He called his assistant, George, whom I also knew. Mayor Lopez asked him, "Tell Art what we were talking about just a moment ago."

George said, "We were talking about professionalizing the police department by hiring younger guys to replace our old political appointees."

Mayor Lopez told George, "Art just requested to join the police department, and he studied criminal justice in the Marines."

George told us, "Go for it."

Mayor Lopez said, "Go to Police Commissioner Ernie Olivas at his grocery store and tell him that I want you employed immediately. I will call Chief Montano and tell him to talk to you. Do you have any other requests or questions?"

"No, sir, only that I would request to be considered for the graveyard shift, since I will be attending school during the day."

He said, "Art, that is where we need you the most, so your request is granted. One more thing. I want you to closely evaluate the status of the department and implement any improvements you consider essential."

"Needless to say, boss, that I will have to do it in a low-profile manner and will coordinate any improvements with your current chief, so he wouldn't think that I'm trying to replace him. Okay?"

"Exactly. You do that. I'm going to authorize a small budget for needed items, so keep me posted. Now go see Ernie."

I drove to Olivas Grocery Store on New Mexico Avenue. I didn't know him personally, only that he was an insignificant fellow in his early thirties.

He was stooped over the cash register counter when I entered and greeted him. He ignored me and continued checking his receipts. I sensed his self-important attitude would not contribute to a gracious meeting.

He finally looked up and in a harsh voice spoke as he pointed his shaking finger at me. "How dare you going over my head to the mayor to solicit for a job in the police department? I'm the police commissioner, and applicants go through the chain of command. Do you understand?"

I probably pissed him off more by smiling while he ranted on. When he finally shut the hell up, I told him, "To start out, Ernie, until a while ago that the mayor told me to come see you to be processed into the police department, I didn't know you or your position existed. If you have any problems with that, I suggest you take it up with the mayor."

His face turned red, and his eyes narrowed as he went through his little tantrum, realizing that he had not rattled my cage at all.

He settled down a bit but continued with his petty harassment. He said, "I know your family is Democrat, and we Republicans are now in control, so if you want the job, you will have to go to the county court clerk's office and have your political affiliation changed to Republican."

I said, "Okay, I'll be right back." I drove a block back on New Mexico Avenue to the San Miguel County Building. Upon entering I was happy to see Ernest Kavanagh working there. He was Tio Joe and Tuddy Kavanagh's brother, and we had always considered ourselves quasi-relatives.

After exchanging hugs and salutations, I told Ernest the purpose of my visit and the confrontation I had with Ernie.

Ernest smiled and said, "Don't worry, *primo* (cousin). We will take care of that." He handed me a political affiliation form. I filled it and retained a copy to show it to Ernie. As I was leaving, Ernest told me, "Once you show it to him, come back here, okay?"

"You got it, *primo*."

I returned to Olivas Grocery Store and handed Ernie the signed form. Apparently while I was gone he had received a second phone call from Mayor Lopez, because his attitude had improved slightly. He instructed me to report to Chief Montano at the police station.

En route to the police station, I stopped at the county clerk's office, and Ernest pointed to the top of the counter without saying a word. I followed his direction to a new political affiliation form making me a Democrat again. I signed it and tore up the previous one. As I walked out I hoped God would forgive me for being a Republican for ten minutes.

At the police station I experienced a nostalgic feeling, remembering the last time I visited this office as a child when I got lost in the Plaza Park. The police station had not changed a bit with the exception that it was dirtier. Officer Abe, whom I recognized as an old timer who owned a small grocery store near North Public School, was sitting behind the single office desk nervously twiddling with a pencil.

After I greeted him, he said, "The chief just called and said that the police commissioner had instructed him to come see you. He was not happy about having to come on his day off."

Shortly afterward, Chief Montano, a heavyset guy in his mid-forties, stormed into the office in a foul mood. Without looking at me, he said, "Isn't this a bitch that I have to come on my day off to see someone who doesn't respect the chain of command?"

I remained standing and speechless, waiting for the chief to stop bitching. He finally calmed down a bit, but continued sarcastically, "You will have to buy your uniform, which is available only in Albuquerque, but for the time being, wear black trousers and shirt. The swing shift officer will leave you his cap and Sam Brown holster and gun. You report to duty at eleven-thirty tonight."

I asked him, "Sir, are there any operating procedures I should familiarize myself with?"

That was the wrong question to ask. He responded, "We dumb cops have nothing to teach you, since I understand you have studied criminal justice. The one thing that I can tell you is that if you screw up, don't expect us dumbasses to bail you out."

He then stormed out of the office.

"Welcome aboard!" I thought to myself as I exited after him. When I got home, Mom told me, "Quick, telephone Tio Joe Kavanagh. He heard from Ernest that the police department hired you."

I called Tio Joe, who told me to come to his house right away. At his home we exchanged greetings realizing that we had not seen each other for several years.

He told me, "Ernest told me about you getting a job in the police department, and I wondered if you had a uniform."

"No, Tio, as a matter of fact I was told to wear a black shirt and trousers until I buy a uniform in Albuquerque."

He said, "Bullshit. Here, come into our bedroom."

I followed him and saw that he had a complete almost- new police uniform laid out on the bed. Besides the uniform he had a black leather police jacket and Sam Brown holster. The shirt even had the official WLV Police cloth patches sewed on.

"I'm giving you the uniform free and will sell you the jacket and Sam Brown belt and holster for twenty bucks, but I don't expect you to pay me now, since you must have other pending expenses."

"No way, Tio," I said as I took out my wallet and gave him twenty dollars.

Besides getting the complete police outfit, he gave me good advice after I told him how the flaky police commissioner and the chief had treated me. He said, "Mayor Lopez is doing a hell of a good job, and he is trying to reform the old system. As long as you have his backing, don't worry about those other guys."

I thanked him and rushed home to get ready for my new job. I ironed my new uniform and spit-shined my shoes and reported to

CHAPTER 5

work that night. When I entered the office, Officer Ortiz, who was the only one there, was talking on the telephone, but when he saw me, dropped the phone, and almost fell as he stood up and asked me, "What's happening?"

I identified myself and explained I had been hired. He responded "Shit. That's right. They told me you would be coming in, but to tell you the truth, when you walked in, I thought you were New Mexico State Police, and they only show up when the shit hits the fan. Besides that, they told me you didn't have a uniform."

He had complimented me on my appearance, claiming that he thought that I was a state cop. After introductions and small talk, I felt confident that my night patrol partner and I would make a good team.

He told me, "Art, I'm going to level with you. I heard about how shitty the chief treated you, and I'm going to tell you why. His whole world is being chief of police, and because of your friendship with the mayor and your police training, he feels his position is in jeopardy. But if you explain to him what you told me about your plans, I can assure you that he will be more civil."

I thanked him for his solid advice, and after chatting for a while and seeing that we had not gone out on patrol, I questioned him about it. He said, "We have only one car, and the car's radio phone is not functional. So if anyone is in trouble, they telephone us. We have to be here to take the calls and respond."

This problem would have to be addressed as a priority. I visited our next-door neighbors, the fire department, and borrowed a bucket and a mop and other cleaning stuff. I removed my shirt and conducted a Marine Corps- type field day washing the floor and windows, as well as the restroom.

The following morning when the chief and Officer Abe arrived, they complimented me for the cleanup job. I took advantage of the moment and asked the chief if I could talk to him in private. He sent Abe on patrol.

"Chief, I only wanted to tell you my law enforcement plans. I want to continue my education at Highlands University and later on, go on to a larger police department."

Officer Ortiz was correct. The chief's immediate response was very positive, and he agreed with my implementing some of my ideas to improve the proficiency of the department, requesting only that I keep him posted on whatever changes I would recommend.

On the following day, I visited the mayor, and he gave me a hundred dollars to buy office and cleaning equipment.

I established a telephone-call ledger identifying the caller, the time and date of the call, and space for the synopsis of the call. This ledger replaced an old yellow-paged notebook with a few unintelligible entries regarding telephone calls received. I also made several forms for documenting criminal activities. I coordinated with District Attorney Donald Tiny Martinez for his approval of the forms I established. I also made a cleanup schedule.

At Highlands I enrolled in Dr. Richard O'Connell's drama English classes. He was a renowned Shakespearian authority, and I played in minor roles in *Hamlet* and other productions.

During one of my extended day shifts, the New Mexico State Police informed us that a male suspect had just pulled a bank robbery at the East Las Vegas Bank.

Chief Montano instructed me to proceed to South Highway 85 and block all cars traveling south at the intersection of Pacific Street. If I saw anything suspicious, I was to telephone our office from the nearby Matias Grocery Store.

I set up the roadblock and started profiling people and searching their vehicle trunks.

An El Paso police officer came by my roadblock, got down from his car, and opened the trunk of his car without being asked, after seeing me check the trunk of the car in front of him. He was most gracious and told me that he had come to visit his girlfriend at Mora, and he would like to help me, but he had to hurry back to the graveyard shift. I thanked him for his offer, telling him I understood his situation.

CHAPTER 5

As soon as he took off, something bothered me about the guy. For one thing, he had no luggage of any kind. I felt that he should have at least have a toilet kit. I also failed to see his weapon, even though he showed me his police credentials.

I telephoned the chief from the nearby store and told him about my suspicions. He told me to stand by while he relayed the information to the state police.

He telephoned me back all excited, telling me, "Art, you hit the jackpot. That's the guy. The state police are on their way to talk to you. Get back to your post."

By the time I got back to my intersection, I could hear several police sirens, and shortly afterward, three of them arrived. When I gave the additional information, including the suspect's Texas license plate number and the suspect's description, they radioed their Santa Fe headquarters office and took off after the suspect.

Later I learned that the suspect had checked his luggage to El Paso, Texas, at the Greyhound depot and at the last moment skipped out of place. The bus clerk had heard about the bank robbery and reported the incident to the state police. The bus clerk and I were subpoenaed to testify at the Federal Court in Albuquerque. The defendant changed his plea to guilty after learning there was no way he could claim his innocence.

A few months later, during the Christmas holidays, my police career came to an abrupt halt. While on patrol at midnight, I observed a vehicle traveling in an erratic manner on Bridge Street. I stopped the apparently drunk female driver and placed her under arrest after issuing her a DWI citation.

She flirted with me, offering sex in exchange for releasing her. I ignored her efforts but told her that in the interest of saving her money, if she could have some relative or friend take her car, I would not have to impound it.

She said, "Thanks, and I have a friend across the street in Joe's bar." I followed her to the bar. She walked in and turned around and

DON'T EXPECT ANYTHING

sarcastically told me, "I want you to see what I'm going to do with the damn ticket you issued me."

She handed the citation to Police Commissioner Ernie Olivas, who was sitting on one of the bar stools. He tore up the citation and hugged and kissed her. The idiot didn't realize that I was standing by the entrance door. When I approached him and asked him why he had torn up the citation, he answered sarcastically, "I'm the police commissioner and absolve her of the charges. Now get the hell out of here and go back to your patrol." It was evident that those two were together earlier at the place.

I thought about charging him with obstructing justice but remembered how the local system worked. Instead I just told him, "You are a dumb son of a bitch, and tomorrow I will submit my resignation, because it's impossible to work under your full-of-shit command." I walked out, and the following day I told the mayor what had taken place. He attempted to persuade me to stay, but I convinced him that it was time for me to move on.

CHAPTER 6

AFTER THE WINTER semester, Dad came to my rescue with a job as a painter's helper with his Atchison Topeka Santa Fe Railroad paint gang. The paint gang was in Albuquerque, and the painters resided in a boxcar converted into a dormitory/kitchenette.

Since we worked in the large roundhouse where the locomotives were serviced during regular working hours, we worked from ten at night to six in the morning. We had breakfast and slept until about four in the afternoon. While Dad and the other painters took it easy during that time frame, I worked out at a local professional boxing gym.

The gym was a small building that contained only a workout room, boxing ring, showers, and lockers. The owner had a mini office in one of the corners.

I paid the twenty-dollar monthly fee after assuring the owner I would comply with the few regulations, including not leaving any sweaty warmups or other stuff in the lockers and providing my own boxing equipment.

Five boxers and their trainer used the gym. Efforts to befriend them were fruitless as they jealously trained by themselves.

A week later I noticed all the boxers were excited about an upcoming boxing event to be sponsored by the famous local wrestling promoter Jack London at the civic auditorium. I approached the boxing managers to see if I could join their stable and be included in the coming event, but they ignored me.

The owner discreetly called me to his office. He told me, "Art, I'm sorry that these guys are not the friendliest in the business, and I don't want them to know what I'm going to tell you. You should talk to Jack London and ask him if he can include you in the event. You will find him at his bar located downtown."

I went to Jack London's bar located a couple of blocks from the railroad station. I recognized him, since he frequently appeared on a TV wrestling program. He resembled Ernest Hemingway, beard and all. He was talking on the telephone.

One of Jack's wrestlers was double dipping as a bartender. I ordered a beer and told him that I would like to talk to Jack. He got me the beer and told Jack my request.

Jack asked me, "What can I do for you, my good man?"

"Sir, my name is Arthur Sedillo, and I just finished a four-year tour as a U.S. Marine varsity boxer and have won several Golden Glove boxing tournaments, including the New Mexico and western United States title, and I want to fight professionally. I understand you're sponsoring a boxing match in a couple of weeks and wondered if you could include me in it."

Jack asked me, "What is your fighting weight?"

"I'm a welterweight, a hundred and forty-seven pounds."

He said, "This may be your lucky day, if you are not bullshitting me."

"Sir, I'm working here at the Santa Fe Railroad paint gang. I have my scrapbook with several articles and photos of my boxing accomplishments. I can get it and show it to you for your verification."

He said, "Okay, kid. Just for the record, you go and get them, because I'm going to tell you something. Did you see me on the telephone a moment ago?"

"Yes, sir."

"Well, that was one of the managers telling me that his welterweight just broke his hand and will not be able to fight. I had already scheduled him to fight Benny Montoya from Denver."

"Sir, I will be right back. I rushed to the train dormitory and returned with my photo album. Jack London paged through it and quickly returned it, assuring me that I was on the card. He told me I was entitled to have two corner men and to come early to the arena on fight night because I would be the first fight.

I quit my painter's helper job to start training. On my way home I experienced mixed feelings, in the sense that I was venturing into a career without the necessary tools. Typically one would have a boxing manager/trainer and several hours of sparring. One would also need professional corner men to assist during the fight. I had none.

To get into shape, I drove daily to the nearby Montezuma Dams and ran up the dirt mountain road to the Gallinas Canyon and back, a distance of approximately six miles. I would then shadow box eight rounds, doubling the four rounds I would be boxing.

My second major problem was coming up with two corner men. I convinced my third cousin Chamo Lopez from Las Vegas and Max Lopez, a college buddy, to play the role of my corner men. Neither had the slightest experience in boxing. Chamo was in his middle thirties and was a humble, hard-working laborer. Max, a former college mate in the drama department, worked as a cosmetologist in Albuquerque.

The night before the fight, Chamo and I traveled to Albuquerque and stayed in a cheap hotel. I had Max join us so I could give them a briefing on the role they would be playing.

I told Max, "Just make believe that you are an actor working for an Oscar. Each time between rounds, you pop into the ring corner and play the role that you are giving me instructions on how to improve my performance. Keep in mind that no one will give a shit what you say and probably can't hear you. You will spread a thin layer of Vaseline over my eyebrows to prevent cuts. Chamo will hand you a plastic bottle of water for me to drink. You have only a minute to do all this. A beeper will sound when ten seconds remain, which is the signal for you to get the hell out of the ring.

"Your role, Chamo, is that when the bell rings, you shove the stool to the corner so I can sit on it. You will give the bottle of water to Max when he asks for it. When the bell rings at the end of the rest period, you pull the chair out of the ring after I stand to resume fighting. Now that is all you guys have to do."

My corner men and I arrived early on the evening of the fight, and I walked them down to the ring to familiarize them with the location of the water bottle, stool, and other stuff needed. We went back to the dressing room, and I wore my U.S. Marine trunks and robe. After telling my seconds to wake me up when the official came for us, I took a nap on a bench.

When we were called and approached the ring, I saw Dad and all of the paint gang sitting in the ringside seats. I also noticed several of my Las Vegas relatives and friends in the audience.

I met my opponent at the center of the ring and saw a shitty smile on his mug. After getting the instructions from the referee, we returned to our corners. At the ring of the bell, I made the sign of the cross and came out fighting.

I knocked out Benny in forty-eight seconds in the first round. When I knocked him out and returned to my corner, Chamo yelled at Max, "What should I do with the stool?"

Max answered, "Stick it up your ass. The fight is over. Art won!"

The three of us laughed and the crowd cheered my performance. Jack London gave me an additional twenty-five dollars. I tried to share my earnings with my helpers, but they refused it. We celebrated at London's bar and then went for a late-night Mexican breakfast on 4th street.

I returned to Highlands University for an additional semester and then slipped out of Las Vegas to Los Angeles, to pursue my professional boxing career.

Baron Von Stumme, the professional boxing manager I had previously met, included me in his boxing stable. After six fights, of which I won four and lost two on split decisions, Baron Von Stumme had a serious conversation with me, after making it a point to introduce me to former Lightweight Champion of the World Lauro Salas.

I talked to Lauro Salas and saw that he was almost incoherent. He was telling me something about his car, but the only thing I understood was something about a Chevrolet. The guy certainly had brain damage.

After this incident, Baron Von Stumme told me, "Art, you are a hell of a fighter, but even when you win, you take a beating. You are too intelligent to be in this business. I don't want you to wind up like Lauro. What I'm proposing is that you help me train the guys. I have just purchased a gym in Santa Ana, California.

I agreed with Baron and helped him train some of his boxers and took care of some of the administrative work. His clients included some Santa Ana policemen, whom I trained.

When I was three months into that job, Mom telephoned me and told me that my dear college buddy, Andrew Salazar, who worked in his father's trucking business, had been killed while working under one of the company trucks. Even though I was not able to attend Andrew's funeral, his premature death had a tremendous impact on me. I found it difficult to accept that such an enthusiastic and joyful life was terminated at such a young age.

Shortly after his death I returned to Las Vegas determined to pursue a law enforcement career. I did visit Andrew's brother and assured him that if I ever got married and had a son, I would name him Andrew.

CHAPTER 7

WHEN I ARRIVED in Las Vegas, Mom was watering the lilac bushes and humming an old favorite song when I tried to sneak up on her, but she sensed me and turned around and squirted me. After laughs and hugs, I told her that I was serious about pursuing a law enforcement career in a bigger department.

She said, "You may want to consider the Santa Fe Police Department. Their Chief Benito Martinez happens to be a distant relative. But be careful in bringing this relationship up, so he doesn't think you are trying to ingratiate yourself with him."

"Mom, you must be psychic. That was the first place I was going to check out. Santa Fe is both close and a charming city."

I drove to the Santa Fe police department. Inside the first-floor foyer I saw a police-recruiting announcement on the bulletin board, and my hopes increased. Inside the police reception area a petite Hispanic female police officer was busy at her desk. Upon seeing me, she asked, "Good morning, sir, can I help you?"

"Good morning to you, officer. I hope I'm not too late in responding to your police-recruitment announcement. I'm from Las Vegas,

New Mexico, and recently heard about it," I lied.

She stood up and handed me an application package as she said, "You just made it. The recruitment was ending this afternoon."

Chief of Police Abe Martinez, A heavyset man in his early sixties, overheard our conversation and asked me to follow him into his office. He told me to sit down and then asked me, "What makes you think that you will qualify to be a Santa Fe policeman?"

"Sir, my name is Arthur M. Sedillo, and I was honorably discharged from the Marines a year ago after serving four years and obtaining the rank of sergeant. While in the Marines I studied criminal justice, and for the past year I was a policeman with the West Las Vegas Police Department. The reason I left that department is that I want to join a more professional police department."

He asked me, "What can you tell me about yourself, family, and so forth?"

I was glad he opened this door and said, "Sir, I'm single, and my family resides in Las Vegas. My mother, Lucy Martinez Sedillo, may be a distant relative of yours, but I'm not mentioning it to ingratiate myself with you. My father's family, as well as Mom's, are law-abiding citizens. I have no police record."

Chief Martinez smiled and said, "Now that you mention about your mother, yes, I recall the relationship, and you are right. That information has no bearing on our selection criteria."

After I favorably responded to a few more questions, the chief said, "Okay, Art, we will make a quick criminal record check on you and have our physician check you out to make sure that you are physically and mentally cleared to be a policeman. Once we get that taken care of and you submit the completed application form, we will accept you into our training police academy session that will start on Monday. Have the police officer that was talking with you finish processing you."

He instructed the officer to telephone Dr. Gonzalez to see if he could squeeze me in for an examination right away, since I was an out-of-town applicant.

She phoned Dr. Gonzalez, and after I filled in the application forms, she told me to rush to the doctor's office around the corner. I did that and passed the examination and returned the needed medical document to be included in my application package.

On March 4, 1962, I checked into a motel on Cerrillos Road, a half block from the New Mexico School for the Deaf, which lent facilities to the police department for training.

Our class of thirteen applicants graduated on a Friday before Easter Sunday, and all except me got the weekend off. Chief Martinez walked up to me after the graduation ceremony and said, "You told me you wanted to be a policeman. Well, I'm going to make sure you become a good one. You report to Captain Alarid at 10:30 p.m. tonight for the graveyard shift. Do you have a problem with that?"

I smiled and saluted him, saying, "Not at all, sir. Thank you."

I reported to work at 10:30 p.m. to Shift Commander Captain Paul Alarid. He was in his early fifties and a bit on the pudgy side and wore thick glasses. After he and I exchanged greetings, the second in command, Lieutenant David Gonzales, a sharp guy in his mid-thirties, joined us. Both men briefed me on my assignment. I had previously met Lieutenant Gonzales in training and was glad to work under his command.

My senior partner, Officer Margarito Maez, and I would patrol together for a month. His monthly evaluation of my performance would determine my permanent status in the department.

The rest of the officers on the shift trickled in, and they were gracious, taking the trouble to come and shake hands, welcoming me.

A patrol car was assigned to me after my successful probation period was confirmed. I continued patrolling the downtown and west side areas.

I was impressed with the department's professionalism but noticed a rivalry among shifts. Our graveyard shift referred to the day shift as the public relations group that spent all its time helping tourists, helping old ladies cross the street, and kissing higher management's ass.

CHAPTER 7

The swing shift, whom we tolerated a bit more, were the traffic cops and ticket givers. We, the graveyard shift, considered ourselves the felon ass kickers, even though the other two shifts referred to us as the department's degenerates.

This self-imposed shift rivalry had positive and negative implications. On the positive side, each shift tried to out-produce the other two. On the downside, some opportunities to coordinate ongoing investigations was compromised on the theory that each shift wanted to take full credit for the case. It was not unusual for one shift to steal a case from the other shift.

For example, on a Sunday morning, I responded to a call to investigate a DWI that had crashed into a residence. At the accident scene, I found the drunk driver and his companion still sitting inside the car that had crashed into the living room of a humble family's home. The family was shocked but thankful that no one was in the living room when the accident occurred.

Both the driver and his friend were laughing, and upon seeing me, the driver said, "We just popped in for a cup of coffee, but these people are not very friendly."

When I handcuffed the men, I noticed a man who told me he was a neighbor and wanted to talk to me in private.

Outside the house the guy told me, "I saw them stash their marijuana under the seat. The family members are my neighbors and dear friends, so please bust those dope heads." I thanked him and returned to the accident scene.

I told the driver, "Before I call the wrecker to tow away your car, I want to take inventory of all you have in the car, because we have had complaints that items have disappeared, and the towing people have been accused of taking them. Before I start checking, is this your car, and is everything in it yours?"

The driver took the car registration from the glove compartment and told me, "Check it out, officer. See how it is registered to me? Yes, everything here is mine."

DON'T EXPECT ANYTHING

I checked the trunk, itemizing the spare tire and other shit. When I got to the inside of the car and checked under the back seat, I pulled out the paper sack containing half a pound of marijuana and told the driver, "As you said, everything in the car is yours."

The driver right away accused his partner. "That shit is not mine; it belongs to this guy.

The other person said, "Bullshit; it's yours. Besides that, you told the officer that everything in the car was yours, so you're fucked." His buddy laughed.

I told them, "Look, so that there will be no hard feelings between you guys, I'm charging you both for possession of marijuana. You, the driver, get an additional charge of DWI, and you, the passenger, is charged with public intoxication, and so to quote you, both of you are fucked."

I arrested them. I had to work four hours past my shift to finish the paperwork and process the evidence.

When I came to work on the following day, I learned that the detectives had taken over my case. Not only did they scam a trip to Albuquerque to have the evidence checked at the laboratory, but they also took credit for the case in the news media. I made it a point to harass them for stealing my case.

On a quiet Sunday night, the dispatcher sent me out of my patrol area to investigate a possible break and entry at an artist shop on Canyon Road. The owner, an elderly woman, resided in the rear portion of her shop.

She told me that she woke up upon hearing what sounded like someone trying to break into the front door. She turned on the lights and heard someone running away. I checked the front door and found fresh nicks and wood chips between the door frame and the door.

The woman asked me to check her backyard, telling me that she also had an empty apartment. I checked that apartment and found no evidence of illegal entry. While finalizing my notetaking, I commented on her charming apartment. She said, "My dear officer, nothing would

CHAPTER 7

make me happier than having you rent it. I will give you a deal you can't refuse."

Before I could tell her that I happened to be shopping for an apartment, she added, "I will charge you only fifty dollars a month, and that will include utilities. I took her up on her deal and moved in the following day. During the daylight I found it even more charming. The front and only door was thick rustic wood probably dating back to the 1800's. Wood beams(*vigas*) supported the roof. A corner fireplace complemented the traditional Santa Fe-style home. Besides the single bedroom/living room, it had a bathroom and a mini kitchen.

Access to the apartment was through a drive-through garage to the backyard. As I settled down, it started to snow. My landlady told me to chop the wood logs stored in the garage for both her and my fireplace.

That evening I cooked potatoes with chopped frankfurters mixed with a can of pork and beans. I topped supper with a cup of coffee as I relaxed in a comfortable rocking chair near the warm fireplace. I dozed off listening to my Dave Brubeck jazz record.

Back on the job, I realized that some of our operational activities might have been considered unorthodox by management, but they unwittingly concurred with our positive results. For example, in the interest of minimizing teenagers' drunk driving accidents or other criminal activity, on weekends we would intensify our patrol on known lover's lanes and seized young people's alcoholic beverages. They would bitch and moan but could count their blessings that we didn't bust their asses and they weren't wiped out and endangering themselves and others.

During these patrols, if we found couples making out, we made sure that the females were there of their own free will. If we suspected that the couples were adulterers, we would warn them that if anything happened to their legal mates, the person they were screwing would be considered a suspect. These couples also bitched and drove out of our jurisdiction.

On weekend nights the jail population increased significantly; therefore, my buddy, Officer Robert (Bob) Dominguez, and I initiated

DON'T EXPECT ANYTHING

a plan to reduce the incarceration and related paperwork. We told the drunk arrestees that their arrest was conditional. At about four in the morning, we would walk the drunks out of the drunk tank to the police station parking yard. Like in my U.S. Marine Corps drill instructor days, I would make them march. Those that failed my command three times would be kicked back into the drunk tank. The ones that passed our test were released. As a rule we made them all pass the test.

The other positive thing about this project was that the majority of these drunks were in the lower to middle economic class. Their failure to report to work on Mondays could compromise their jobs, causing their families to be further impoverished.

On Sunday mornings we would take the confiscated liquor to one of our vehicles, and we would go out and party until noon at Hyde Park.

CHAPTER 8

ON SUNDAY EVENING, July 22, 1962, while I was patrolling on the northeast section of Santa Fe, a lavender Triumph sports car ran a stop sign at the intersection of Buena Vista and College Streets. I evaded hitting the car by swerving out of the violator's path.

Angrier than hell, I made a fast U-turn and stopped the female offender. I was stunned by her beauty but maintained my composure. While I reprimanded her and checked her driver's license, she said. "Officer, I'm sorry. I'm a telephone operator here in town but just received an emergency message to cover the Los Alamos office, and I'm running late."

Usually I don't cave in situations like this, but I gave her only a verbal warning to be more careful. Her previous pissed demeanor mellowed a bit as she gave me a sweet smile, thanked me for not citing her, and promised to drive more carefully.

The following morning while having breakfast at Pansy's Café, a state policeman joined me and said, "You should have seen the accident I just finished investigating. A beautiful girl driving a sports car flew right off the highway embankment on a curve of the Los Alamos highway. She went straight down the canyon about fifty yards, and I don't know how she survived."

I stopped eating and took out my notebook and asked him, "By any chance was the car a lavender Triumph, and was her name Mariana?"

The trooper told me, "How in the hell did you know that? The accident took place way the hell out of your jurisdiction, and I don't think it has been released to the press yet. Do you have radar up your ass, or what?"

When he finished blabbing, he did confirm that the victim was named Mariana and that she was recovering at the Los Alamos Hospital. I quickly finished breakfast and rushed home and changed into a clean uniform and drove in my car to the Los Alamos Hospital.

At the hospital, the receptionist amusingly looked at me, probably wondering what the hell a Santa Fe policeman was doing there. I identified myself and asked to see Mariana. She asked me if I was a relative. I told her I wanted to verify if she was the same person I had cited the previous evening. She gave me directions to her room but cautioned me to keep it short because she was still recovering.

As I approached Mariana's bed, I noticed her bruised face. Not knowing how to address her, I came out with the most asinine remark and said, "I'm so sorry I didn't give you a ticket for running the stop sign last night."

Apparently still in pain and a bit drowsy, she responded, "You are crazy if you think you are going to give me a ticket now."

I felt like an idiot and quickly raised my hands in surrender and added, "No, I'm sorry. What I meant to say is that maybe if I had issued you the citation, you would have been more careful this morning, and you wouldn't have been involved in a horrible accident."

She must have realized my sincerity, because she appeared to smile. I wished her a quick recovery and departed.

As I drove back to Santa Fe, I had a pleasant sensation that it was not going to be the last time I would see her. As a kid I was a bit shy when it came to the opposite sex. I remember having a crush on a few girls, but most of them ignored me or the relationship didn't go beyond being "only friends."

I knew that I would have to get to know Mariana better and ask her for a date. After contemplating how to approach her, I decided to just go for it cold turkey.

My buddy, Officer Bobby Dominguez, told me that he had known Mariana since their high school days and assured me that she was a wonderful person. He strongly supported me in getting to know her.

Three weeks later Bobby and I walked into the Sombrero Café downtown and saw Mariana sitting with several of her female friends. Bobby formally introduced me to her. Like an idiot, right off the bat, I asked her to go on a date with me. She responded, "I don't even really know you, and I think you are pretty brassy in asking me for a date."

I apologized.

Her smile gave me hope to continue pursuing her. Later I learned that she had asked Officer Belinda about my character and if I was single. Officer Belinda apparently gave her a positive report, because the next time I asked her for a date, she agreed.

I picked her up at her residence and jokingly told her I was going to take her out to eat a big steak, knowing that she was still recovering from her jaw injury and was eating only soft foods.

We stopped at a fast food place where she ordered a light soup and salad, and I munched on a cheeseburger and fries. After that I drove her to my hometown, West Las Vegas, pointed out my parents' house, and returned to Santa Fe.

When I left her at her residence, I had not even kissed her or laid a finger on her. I told her, "Someday you are going to be my wife."

She answered, "I'm not looking for a husband, and if I were, you are not it."

Three months later we were married at the Santa Fe Cathedral on my twenty-fifth birthday, February 2, 1963. It was the happiest day of my life. I moved out of my apartment to her residence on Buena Vista

Street, the same location where she almost ran into me on our first encounter.

Besides falling in love with Mariana, I fell in love with her two young daughters from a previous marriage, Athena and Rita, and officially adopted them.

Being in love escalated my lifestyle to a higher plane. I always thanked God for bringing Mariana into my path.(No pun intended.) My previous life was at best mundane. Mariana, without a doubt, improved my physical, psychological, and spiritual life.

A couple of months later, Mariana changed jobs and went to work at the New Mexico State Motor Vehicle Department at the state capitol. Because of our conflicting work schedules, I had to practice the virtue of patience. When I got home in the mornings, I wanted to cuddle up to her, but since she was preparing to go to work, she would stiff-hand me like a football running back, telling me to be patient until the weekend.

Mariana's Aunt Rita, who owns the house where we were residing, was the caretaker, maid, and cook for the famous author Witter Bynner. His estate and where she lived was across the street from us. Aunt Rita and her assistant, Lucinda Gurule, helped us take care of our preschool daughters.

Unfortunately shortly after our wedding, Tia Rita had a stroke and was in a coma for about a month before she died. A few days before she died I started house hunting without consulting Mariana, knowing that once Tia Rita died, the house would be part of her estate and would be sold.

A fellow policeman told me of a real nice three-bedroom house for sale right next to his on Salazar Street. I checked it out and loved it. On the weekend I drove Mariana and the girls to the house I had bought. When we got there, I told them. "Welcome to your new home."

Mariana thought I was kidding until my fellow policeman and his wife came out of their house and welcomed us to our new home. Mariana started crying, and I didn't know if her tears were of joy or fear, wondering how in the hell were we going to pay for the house.

Once she checked out the inside, she agreed that this was a must thing, but still admonished me, stating, "You have to promise never to commit to any other expense like this without consulting with me first." Within the same breath, she admitted loving it and broke out in a big smile and kissed me.

Mariana continued impressing me. This was not limited to me. At her State Capitol Motor Vehicle job she quickly advanced through the secretarial ranks and became Motor Vehicle Commissioner Benny Sanchez's executive secretary.

After two more years on the job, I realized that it was time to move on. I loved my job but at the same time recognized the limited opportunities for advancement. I was no longer alone and needed to strive to better provide for my family.

I discussed my feeling with Mariana, and she agreed that I should apply to the New Mexico State Police. Several other Santa Fe police officers also applied, but we all did it discreetly, knowing that Chief Martinez would fire any officer that applied to the New Mexico State Police.

The six other city police applicants agreed that I train them in getting into good physical condition in preparation for the NMSP training seminar. We heard several rumors that it was almost as tough as the USMC boot camp.

While I was training the guys, Abe, whose uncle was one of few Hispanic state policeman, told me, "Art, I don't want to discourage you, but unless Hispanic applicants have a strong political connection or relative in the state police, your chances of being hired are nil."

I didn't give much weight to the rumor and continued with our workouts. Two weeks later when the announcements were made, all the guys I had been training were called except me. They all had the connections Abe had told me.

When I got home from that last workout, I told Mariana. We both broke down in tears and she sympathized with me. On the following day, which was my day off, Mariana came home from work with a big smile. I asked her, "What's up?"

She didn't tell me anything until we received a telephone call, and she told me, "Honey, my boss, Mister Sanchez, wants to talk to you."

I had attended several motor vehicle training seminars and social activities that Mariana had invited me to attend and had previously befriended Mr. Sanchez. I got on the phone and greeted the motor vehicle commissioner. "Good afternoon, sir. How are you?"

"Just fine, Art. I just wanted to tell you that Mariana told me about your not being included in the NMSP recruitment session. Well, I telephoned Chief Black, and he assured me that you would be included in the upcoming class. You will be getting a phone call from his office to confirm your appointment and give you additional details."

I told him, "Sir, I just don't know how to thank you, but I assure you that I will not let you down."

"I know, Art, and I have no doubt that you will be an outstanding state police officer. You have a good day."

"Thank you, sir." I hung up the phone and grabbed Mariana, hugged and kissed her thanking her for getting Mr. Sanchez to become my NMSP rabbi.

Shortly after, I received another telephone call. "Mr. Arthur Sedillo, I'm Captain Bill Draggers with the NMSP. I'm calling to inform you that you have been selected as a candidate to attend our upcoming police academy training session."

Acting surprised I answered, "Thank you very much, sir."

He gave me instructions regarding my reporting date to the training session at the Glorieta Pass Baptist Camp located approximately twenty-five miles east of Santa Fe.

A week later, Mariana drove me to the training session. My fellow police officers were surprised to see me. Capt. Draggers, a six foot-plus heavy set man, opened the orientation session that included assignment of room partners and other housekeeping and training duties. He told us that we would have physical training and classes from six in the morning until nine at night.

At the end of the first session, several of the candidates walked up to Captain Draggers and introduced themselves. I got in line to do the same, but after I introduced myself, not only did he ignore me, but he even sidestepped me to greet the candidate behind me. I felt embarrassed and wondered what motivated the man to act in such a manner.

At six in the morning our physical training officer, Sergeant Mauricio Cordova, a former U.S. Marine, had us running several laps around the campus on the snow-packed dirt road. After that, we worked out in the gym for an additional half hour. At the conclusion of the training session a month later, I felt confident that I had excelled in both physical and classroom courses. Sergeant Cordova discreetly told me that he was going to try to have me assigned to his post in Albuquerque, New Mexico.

In preparation for our graduation ceremony, Captain Draggers informed us that the class president would be selected from one of the top two candidates, which included me. I thought it was strange and wondered why he didn't just pick the number-one guy.

Instead both of us finalists were instructed to give a spontaneous speech regarding why we wanted to be state police. When the captain added that we should both speak at the same time, I knew that it was a setup to eliminate me.

The other candidate, a hell of a nice Anglo guy, just looked at me, wondering what the hell was going on. We started speaking as instructed, and shortly after, my honorable competitor stopped, while I continued. When I finished and received applause from the class, Captain Draggers changed his mind and said we would have a vote to see who won. Again my competitor and I were puzzled. After the vote, pieces of paper placed in a hat, the captain counted them by himself and stated my opponent had won. I had no doubts the guy had discriminated against me, but as a minority rookie, I thought it best not to complain.

Mariana picked me up after the graduation, and we celebrated with

DON'T EXPECT ANYTHING

one of her outstanding suppers and topped it off with a bottle of economic champagne.

The following morning I got my assignment to report to duty at the Albuquerque District Office. To further complement our relocation, Mariana was also transferred to the Albuquerque State Motor Vehicle Department.

My immediate supervisor, Sergeant Jameson, briefed me on the presence of my senior patrol partner, Officer Jack Johnson. I would be riding shotgun with Johnson for a month to familiarize myself with the patrol area before I was cut loose.

Our patrol area extended from the Albuquerque southwest city limits to the Los Luna County line. The district included several communities and the Isleta Pueblo. Because of the demographics of the area, our patrol would be more like that of metropolitan police, rather than the usual state police duties of patrolling the highways.

Once a week I would be patrolling by myself because of the other officer's day off. On those days, after my regular tour of duty, I would drive home way the hell out in northwest Albuquerque. In the event a call came in while I was back home, I had to rush back to my patrol area.

After a few of those calls, I realized that I was not only jeopardizing my safety speeding to my zone, but also my delay in responding could compromise the safety of victims.

After one of those runs, I stopped at Jerry's Market located in Los Padillas, the last village in my area that borders the Isleta Indian Reservation. I expressed my dilemma to the store owner, Jerry Jaramillo, whom I had befriended after learning that he was a concerned community leader. He was in his late forties, tall and slender, and wore round rimless glasses. Each time I saw him, he appeared to be in a happy mood.

Jerry told me, "You know what, Art? We have never had a state policeman reside here in Los Padillas. As soon as you finish your soft drink, jump into your car and follow me across the street."

CHAPTER 8

I followed Jerry a block down Las Milpas Street to a practically new residential area. He stopped in front of the last house on the block. It has about half an acre of cultivated land that was bordered by an irrigation ditch. Several large cottonwood trees bordered the continuing road for about half a mile to the Rio Grande. Behind the houses across the street started the Isleta Pueblo Reservation property.

I followed Jerry into a practically new, beautiful three-bedroom house. The kitchen had new appliances, and the master bedroom had a wall-to-wall fireplace. I didn't know what Jerry had in mind, but I knew that the house was beyond my pay scale.

Jerry said, "Art, this house was recently built by a friend of mine, but after a bad divorce, he moved out, and I bought it from him. It is not moving, and I can rent it to you at a reasonable price."

When he offered it at a price lower than what I was currently paying, I told him that before I committed, I would have to bring my wife and show it to her.

The following day I drove Mariana and the kids to check out the house. As expected they loved it, and that same day we became Los Padillas residents.

CHAPTER 9

THE MAJORITY OF the Los Padillas adults were hardworking lower- to middle-class people who commuted to work in Albuquerque. Because of this situation, most of the juveniles were unsupervised and tended to get into trouble, especially in the summer months.

Right across from Jerry's Market was an abandoned Catholic Church building. Each time I drove by the area, several of the kids would be sitting on the front steps of the church, and they would greet me by extending their middle finger.

Instead of getting pissed off, I thought back to my problematic youth and just acknowledged their greeting by also flipping the finger back at them, accompanied by a smile.

In the evening I started parking my police unit in front of the abandoned church and saw that the kids didn't like my infringing on their turf.

The reason I parked there late in the evenings was that across the street near Jerry's Market was a bar. The drunk patron Indians from the Isleta Pueblo staggered across the street, resulting in injuries and even deaths.

If I arrested them and took them all the way downtown to the Albuquerque County Jail, I would leave my area unprotected for a considerable time; therefore, I dumped the drunk Indians in my back seat and dropped them off at their homes. I chewed their asses out, telling them that I was not their taxi service. The satisfaction that I got was that once I dropped them off at the Indian Reservation, their wives beat the shit out of them.

The only problem with my practice was that each Sunday morning after the night that I had dumped those guys at their homes, their wives dropped baskets with pumpkins, chili peppers, corn, and other vegetables at my front door. I kept telling them we were prohibited from accepting any gratuities. They responded, "We don't know what you are talking about, Mr. Policeman."

In the interest of reducing juvenile delinquency, I came up with an idea of converting the abandoned church into a recreation hall. I asked Jerry Jaramillo about the status of the building. He told me that it belonged to the Catholic Church under the control of Monsignor Stadtmueller, who resides at the Isleta Pueblo Catholic Church. I told Jerry about my idea, and he agreed to help me form a club.

I visited Monsignor Stadtmueller at the Isleta Catholic Church, and after pleasantries, I told him, "Monsignor, I'm concerned about the increased juvenile delinquency in Los Padillas and attribute it in part to the lack of recreational facilities. Jerry Jaramillo informed me that the abandoned church is under your stewardship. I was wondering if you would permit us to convert it into a recreational hall for the kids."

Monsignor responded without hesitation, "I think that would be an excellent idea. You have my permission and blessing to use it, but prepare me a notary-public-certified document that the church will not be liable for any injuries."

I reported the good news to Jerry, and we had the justice of the peace notarize a document per the monsignor's request. The following Sunday morning, while the monsignor had Mass at our Los Padillas

DON'T EXPECT ANYTHING

village church, I handed the document to him. Monsignor Stadtmueller told the congregation at Sunday Mass about our proposed program and asked the public to support and assist us in carrying out the project.

We also solicited assistance from local and downtown businessman. A furniture store owner donated us a pool table and two ping-pong tables. His only request was that his donation be anonymous. He said that as a kid he was a hell-raiser and he thanked God for a Boy's Club, where he had cleaned up his act.

The pool table became such a big hit that we had to log a schedule on our makeshift bulletin board; otherwise, the bullies controlled it.

We had a meeting with the parents at the converted boys club, and Mariana suggested that we sponsor a Mexican dinner to raise money for needed items. Several of the community women got involved, and we made a couple hundred dollars.

We used some of the money to buy boxing equipment. I explained to the guys that from then on, if they had any misunderstanding among themselves, they would settle it in the boxing ring instead of street fighting, which resulted in injuries and grudges.

To start the boxing program, without telling them about my boxing background, I told them, "If anyone of you wants to knock the heck out of a policeman without being arrested, I will give you that opportunity right now to come and box with me."

Just as I expected, an eighteen-year-old bully smirked as he raised his hand, telling me, "Wow, I'll take you up on that."

As we both put on the boxing gloves, I instructed the rest to form a human ring around my opponent and me. We got a timekeeper to bang a bucket with a broomstick to indicate the end of the two-minute round.

My opponent was shocked when I kept slipping his haymaker punches and countered with mine. In less than a minute he had been humiliated enough, and I stopped the bout. I explained to him and the rest that I had taken advantage of my opponent by not telling them about my previous boxing background. My opponent felt vindicated

CHAPTER 9

for his bad performance and agreed to become our assistant boxing trainer.

A few weeks later I received a call to proceed to the bar across from our recreational hall. When I got there, several kids were standing outside of the bar. Lalo, my assistant trainer, said, "We are here to help you knock the shit out of those Barelas troublemakers that are fighting in the bar."

I was touched how the same guys who enjoyed flipping me their middle finger were volunteering to help me break up a fight. I told them, "You guys will never know how much I appreciate your offer to help me, but unfortunately you are too young to make you my posse, and I would get into trouble by permitting you underage guys into the bar."

Lalo opened the door and yelled to the men inside, "Officer Sedillo is coming in here to break up the fight, and if any of you touch him, we will kick the shit out of you."

When I walked into the bar, the fighting stopped, and all local and Barelas gangsters had their hands up, letting me know the fight was over. The bar owner complained that several chairs and glasses had been broken.

Before I could respond, one of the Barelas guys got out a wad of dollar bills and peeled off a one-hundred-dollar bill and handed it to the bar owner.

All the suspects walked out and saw the kids standing by outside and continued to their cars with their hands up and got the hell out of the area. I thanked the kids again and exchanged high fives with them.

Sometime after, on my day off, I ran the one block from my house to the recreational hall. One of the older guys was sitting on the front steps waiting for me to talk in private.

He told me, "Now I don't want you to think that I'm a snitch. It's that I'm pissed that while you are busting your ass to help the guys over here, some dopers are pushing heroin on them. Now they started pushing that shit on my younger brother, and he almost overdosed."

DON'T EXPECT ANYTHING

I said, "Listen to me, the furthest thing in my mind is thinking of you as a snitch. I consider you a concerned citizen, and I can assure you that I will do everything within my power to bust those dope pushers. All I will need is a bit more information on identifying them, and I'll take it from there."

"It's not just that I'm a concerned citizen, but I thought that I'd better tell you before I take it into my own hands and kill those sons of bitches."

"You did the right thing by coming to me," I told him. "What I need now is to have them identified."

"I don't know their names, but the main one is nicknamed Pelon (baldy) because he is completely bald. They live in Barelas, and I can get the address."

"No, just give me a more-or-less location of their house, and I will find it."

"It's the second to last house on Barelas Lane that ends near a dirt path to Isleta Boulevard. They have an old car seat in front of their shit hole. They sit there, drink beer, and do drugs while they are eyeballing for the police in case they are about to make a sale. Pelon has a 1964 primer-black Chevrolet with a hopped-up engine."

"You have provided me with enough information. I will take it from there. Thanks, guy."

"Wait, one more thing. My kid brother told me they get their shit from some old bitch in Juarez, Mexico, they call La Nacha."

"That is great. Now don't do anything stupid. Just give me the opportunity to take care of it."

"Okay, man."

I met with Sergeant Cordova and obtained his permission to pursue the Pelon investigation. He told me, "Okay, Art, you can do the preliminary investigation to the point that you confirm the identification of the suspects. Once you have this done, I will have you coordinate your investigation with Lieutenant Sosa and his narcotics unit. Okay?"

"You got it, Jefe."

CHAPTER 9

On my own time, I checked out the suspect's residence, which was easy to find. I dressed in Levi's, a white T-shirt, cheap sunglasses, and an old baseball cap. I located the suspect's house and got the house address and suspect's vehicle license plate number. On my first surveillance, I didn't see anyone.

For the entire week, I walked the area in the morning and afternoons to give the impression that I resided in the nearby area and took this route to work. On Wednesday afternoon two guys were sitting on the old car seat that was in front of the house. They were talking to someone inside the house through the opened door. The suspects didn't pay attention to me walking to the nearby dirt path.

On Friday morning, the same two guys were sitting on the car seat drinking coffee. They were arguing with Pelon, who was servicing his car engine.

I heard Pelon yelling at the other two suspects, "Get off your fucking asses and come help me. We don't have that much time."

One of the guys sitting in the car seat responded, "What's your rush? The bitch will take care of us whenever we get there."

None gave a shit about me walking by, since they had seen me before and even exchanged hand-waved greetings. I had no doubts that the female they had referred to was La Nacha in Juarez, Mexico.

I relayed this information to Sergeant Cordova, and he instructed me to proceed to the office and coordinate the information with the Narcotics Unit. I had prepared a preliminary report and rushed to the narcotics office.

I met with Sergeant Cordova and Lieutenant Sosa as well as Narcotics Agent George Ulibarri, and after submitting my findings, I was instructed to go home and change into civilian clothing and stand by for Agent Ulibarri to pick me up. We would be setting up surveillance near the Indian Reservation to see if the suspects traveled south.

Albuquerque Police Narcotics Agents Manny Aragon and Charlie Brown were contacted to assist us. They would discreetly check the suspect's house to determine when they headed south.

I rushed home and changed. George picked me up, and we parked under the cottonwood trees on the highway rest area adjacent to the Isleta Pueblo. Half an hour later, the Albuquerque narcos radioed us that they were following the suspect car and three occupants south on Isleta Boulevard.

When I saw the black-primer Chevrolet approaching, I got all excited, telling George, "That's it. That's it, man!" The police department narcos discontinued their surveillance when we replaced them. We followed the suspects past the Isleta Reservation and onto the Los Lunas Country line. By all indications they appeared to be on their way to Juarez, Mexico, so we discontinued the surveillance.

George dropped me off at my house, telling me he would pick me up at 6:00 p.m. to continue our surveillance.

We returned to our same location that afternoon near the Isleta Reservation. There was a gentle breeze, so we kept the windows open. George was deep into a paperback mystery, while I maintained surveillance of the northbound traffic. While there was still light, I enjoyed watching Indian kids playing soccer in the lot beyond the rest area.

I tried to get George to tell me more about the Narcotics Unit job description and stories, but he kept it to a minimum, telling me that it was long hours of surveillance.

Late that night George told me, "See how it is not like a walk in the park? It is long hours of surveillance." He also told me that if nothing happened by noon, we would call the operation off.

At about ten in the morning, while George was taking a nap, I yelled at him, "There they come!"

He woke up, and we alerted our police department partners and followed the suspects at a safe distance.

When they reached their house, we regrouped with the police department narcos and agreed that two of us would go to the rear door and the other two would go in through the front door.

After knocking on the door and getting no response, we announced ourselves as police and charged into the house through both sides of the house.

The first good sign was that we found two tequila bottles on the table and noticed that the Texas liquor tax stamp was sealed on them, establishing that they had obtained the bottles in Mexico and had them stamped at the U.S. border side by Texas officials.

We served the residents with the search warrant and made them sit on the sofa while we searched for the heroin. We searched all over, with negative results. I started to get discouraged.

Manny Aragon and I took a cigarette break and went outside and sat in the car seat. Just as we were about to relax, we heard Police Department Agent Charlie Brown yell, "Well, all right!" We rushed inside and found him holding two prophylactics filled with two ounces of heroin. He found them under a loose floorboard in the closet. The guys were booked and later prosecuted on felony charges of possession with intent to sell narcotics.

A few days later, my Los Padillas source of information walked up to me at the recreation hall and gave me a high five, telling me he had read the newspaper article concerning the arrest of Pelon and his associates.

After the initiation of this case, I knew that my destiny was to become a narcotics agent. Unfortunately the NMSP police policy indicated that a patrolman had to have five years of service before they could transfer to the detective or narcotics division.

I kept pestering Sergeant Cordova to let me pursue other narcotic-related investigations. I told him about the guy that claimed to be an informant for the Bernalillo sheriff's office but would instead work with me regarding suspects selling heroin. He was willing to introduce me to them in my undercover capacity.

Sergeant Cordova authorized me only to make a preliminary undercover contact with the suspects to determine if in fact the suspects were for real. He told me, "Once you establish that they are selling heroin, we will coordinate the investigation with the narcotics unit.

You should call the narcotics unit so they can cover you during your meeting with the suspects."

"Yes, sir."

On the evening that the informant agreed to introduce me to the suspects, I telephoned the narcotics office but was informed that no one was available to cover me.

That evening, before the meeting, I stopped at Justice of the Peace Garcia's office and telephoned the informant to meet me at the bar on Barelas Street where he would introduce me to the suspects.

Judge Garcia overheard my phone conversation with the informant and told me, "Art, pardon me for eavesdropping on your conversation, but what weapon are you taking with you?"

I told him I was taking my snub-nose, since the state police-issued regular 38 caliber was too bulky.

Judge Garcia said, "No way. Here, I will lend you my smaller automatic. It will fit better behind your belt, and it has a secret safety." He showed me how to operate the safety, and I agreed to use his pistol instead. I left mine with him.

I still had some time before the meeting, so I stopped at the other justice of the peace office where my friend Joe Medina worked as a mechanic. I would leave my police car there so he could service it while I made contact with the suspects.

When I told Joe where I was going, he said. "Do you have someone backing you up or something like that?"

I told him, "I telephoned the Narcotics Office, and no one was available to cover me."

Joe said, "Bullshit, man. I'll cover you. Just tell me what to do."

I thought for a while and said. "You know what? You are right. Look, I'll give you five bucks, and you show up at the bar a few moments before me and sit on a counter bar stool for better observation. Order a beer and check out the guys in the place. Once I get in, I will meet with the informant and the suspects. All I'm going to do is talk shit with them and not commit myself to buy dope at this time. I'll make plans for a follow-up meeting with them, at which time I will have the narcos covering me. Okay?"

"You got it."

Joe went to the bar before me, and when I got there, the informant was there. I ordered a beer, and we talked while we waited for the suspects. After waiting about half an hour, I concluded that the informant was full of shit and left the bar after discreetly signaling Joe to follow me.

Joe joined me shortly after and we ran into four guys, two of which may have been in the bar we had just left. One of them came right out and asked me, "We understand that you are looking for some *chiva* (heroin)."

The first thing that came to my mind was that maybe they were the suspects that I was going to meet, and they, like me, thought the informant was a loser, and they decided to contact me alone. I told the suspect, "I don't know where you got that information. I'm not interested in buying any right now, but if you can show me your stuff, perhaps I will consider it later on."

The guy talked to his friends and then told me, "Okay, man, we will show you what we have, but it's over there in our car parked in the irrigation ditch. Come, and we will show it to you."

Joe and I followed the four guys, and the one that I was talking to opened the car trunk, and instead of showing me drugs, he quickly took out a tire metal tool and hit me on the head while his partners jumped and started beating Joe.

My boxing instincts kicked in, and I hit the guy in front of me with a hard left hook to his jaw, knocking him to the ground. Unfortunately his partners came to his rescue and started beating on me and stabbing me with a knife. At the same time, they were hitting Joe.

By then it was dark. The pistol I was carrying fell out of my belt and the suspect that I had knocked down, got it and attempted to shoot me in the face. Good thing that he was stupid and didn't know how to disengage the safety, so he used the gun to bang on my face.

DON'T EXPECT ANYTHING

At that very moment I thanked God and Judge Garcia. If I had kept my 38 caliber snub-nosed pistol, I would have been killed, since it did not have a safety. To stop him from hitting me, I faked that I was unconscious or dead.

I heard the other guys that were beating Joe yell, "This one is dead. Let's get the hell out of here."

The guys that were beating me answered, "So is this one. Yes, let's go."

They got into their car and left. After they departed, I called out to Joe. My pain was more emotional than physical, thinking that they had killed Joe, leaving his wife a widow and six lovely children orphaned.

I kept yelling, "Joe, Joe, Joe."

The happiest moment I experienced that evening was hearing Joe's response. "Art, Art, are you okay?"

We both crawled up to the irrigation road and hugged each other, carefully realizing we were both battered. Because of the darkness, we were unable to determine the extent of our injuries but were glad to have survived.

We crossed a barbed wire fence and walked about fifty yards to a house. The door to the house had a window on top, and we could see the light behind the thin cotton curtain. We knocked, but no one answered. Finally a man and his wife in their forties approached the window, moved the curtain sideways, and saw our bloody faces. Their fear was visible, and the man indicated they didn't want to get involved.

I removed my State Police badge from inside my boot and flashed it on the window, telling the people, "We are with the New Mexico State Police, and some thugs have tried to kill us. Please call the police and an ambulance."

The wife told her husband, "Quick, open the door." They opened it and let us in. All I remember from that point on was lying down on the floor and the woman placing a wet towel on my bloody face. I passed out.

Next thing I remember, I was in an ambulance lying down, and Joe was sitting by me, wiping blood from my face with a wet cloth. Fear was all over his face.

I told him, "Joe, you are removing the blood from my face that is falling from yours. Move the hell to the side."

In spite of our pain, we both burst out laughing, and he told me, "You will not believe it. I have already counted twelve police cars from the state, city, and county rushing to where we were assaulted. I gave them the license number you told me and described the suspects to the police."

When we got to the hospital emergency room, the doctor performed surgery near my right eye, assuring me there was no damage to the eye itself. Joe's wounds were also stitched up, and the doctor assured him that his injuries were not life threatening.

While lying on the emergency table, I told the medical personnel not to call my wife, because she was pregnant with our first son. I didn't want to cause her complications. I would telephone her as soon as possible.

While this was going on, a Bernalillo County deputy sheriff friend of mine tapped me on the shoulder and asked me, "Art, can you open your good eye and identify this thug?"

I opened my right eye, turned around, and saw the main guy that had assaulted me. I told the deputy that the man appeared to be the leader. The deputy told me that all four had been arrested and that my gun had been recovered. He added that the other suspects were in the other emergency room.

I telephoned Mariana and gave her a minimized version of what happened, but she didn't go for it and came to the hospital immediately to check me out. Once she saw I was not critical, she chewed my ass out for going without an official backup and for putting poor Joe and his family in jeopardy.

While I was recuperating in the hospital, Captain T. J. Chavez and Sergeant Cordova came to visit me. I heard Captain Chavez tell Sergeant Cordova, "We have to transfer him to the Narcotics Unit

DON'T EXPECT ANYTHING

before he gets himself killed."

I assured them that I was okay and should be back on the job in a couple of days. Sergeant Cordova told me, "Not with that banged-up face. You take it easy for a few days."

The suspects spent a couple of months in jail, and after the trial they received a suspended aggravated assault sentence and were placed on probation. Unconfirmed information reflected the father of one of the defendants had contributed significantly to the judge's election.

When that assault took place I was naïve in the sense that I could not determine why it took place. The suspects' motive certainly wasn't to rob us, because with the exception of the pistol, nothing was taken.

After recuperating, I attempted to locate the alleged informant and learned from his landlord that he had moved out of state. The Bernalillo sheriff's office told me no one knew him. He had claimed that he had worked with them.

Later on I came to the conclusion that the informant in the incident was not an informant as claimed but was used by the assault suspects to showcase me at the bar so they could subsequently kill me in revenge for having Pelon and associates arrested and imprisoned.

CHAPTER 10

TO QUOTE SHAKESPEARE: "Cowards die many times before their death. The valiant never taste of death but once." Instead of licking my wounds and crawling into a comfort zone, I was further motivated to become a narcotics agent.

My hopes increased when Sergeant Cordova told me that the Criminal Division board would be meeting to evaluate if they can transfer me to the narcotics unit in spite of my not having the required five years in service.

I reported to the reviewing board and responded to questions regarding my law enforcement experience and related activities. I was then asked to step out of the conference room while they deliberated.

Shortly after, Sgt. Cordova came for me and his shitty smile was a good sign. Inside the conference room, Criminal Division Chief, Cpt. T.J. Chavez congratulated me for being accepted into the Narcotic Unit. After I thanked the board, Lt. Sosa, my new boss tells me. "Art, welcome aboard. Turn in your police unit and take the black Dodge Charger parked behind the office.

Sgt. Cordova added, "Go home and put your uniform in mothballs in case you change your mind and want to come back to patrolling." Before returning home, I stopped at the Motor Vehicle Department Office to give Mariana a last chance to see me in uniform.

I went home, changed into civilian clothing and returned to the narcotics office. Sosa gave me a general briefing about the unit's operational procedures, then had me review some investigative files for my familiarization.

Lieutenant Jess Sosa was in his early forties and had a slender build and olive complexion. Many would say that his prematurely gray hair was attributed to supervising the wayward four-man unit. He was a suave and super intelligent individual and the only state police officer with a Ph.D. in criminology.

On April 29, 1965, Mariana woke me up and told me, "Honey, we have to go to the hospital; the baby is ready to join us. I jumped out of bed, and before I knew it, ran to the bathroom and shaved off my beard and mustache, which I had carefully been manicuring for my undercover persona.

I rushed Mariana to the Albuquerque hospital and stood by until late that afternoon when our son Andrew Carlo was born. That day definitely was the second happiest day of my life, our wedding being the first. When I first saw my son through the visitor's showcase window, tears of joy filled my eyes. The biggest thrill came shortly after, when I was able to hold him in my arms.

I kissed Mariana and let her rest until she and our son were released and I took them home. I helped rock Andrew to sleep in my arms as I sang the only song I knew, the U.S. Marine Corps hymn, "Halls of Montezuma."

Back on the job, I received a telephone call from a friend, former NMSP Officer Thurman Babbs, who was now a U.S. Secret Service agent stationed in Albuquerque. He said, "Hey Art, I heard that you had made it into the narcs unit. Congratulations for being accepted with those other shit birds."

"Thanks, and screw you. Are you babysitting the president's family dog or what?"

"No, shit for brains, I'm calling you to see if you can accompany me on an undercover gig. I'm going to buy some funny money from a suspect and thought that if a sleazy Chicano accompanies me, it will go smoother. Can you ask your boss if you can make it?"

"He is right here. Let me ask him."

Lieutenant Sosa told me to go for it and added that it was the first time the Secret Service had asked for our assistance.

I picked up Thurman at the Federal Building, and we drove to a white dilapidated wood-frame house behind First Street. The suspect had instructed Babbs to come through the rear entrance. In route to the location, we established our undercover story that we were brothers-in-law.

When we arrived, the suspect was sitting on the wooden steps leading to the rear entrance. Babbs introduced me, and we exchanged handshakes and greetings.

Babbs and the suspect talked shop and exchanged a few counterfeit twenty-dollar bills for real dollars. They agreed to meet for a future larger transaction.

After we left, I kept teasing Babbs that buying funny money was as easy as making patty cakes. Babbs thanked me for accompanying him as he flipped me the finger when I dropped him off at his office.

Three weeks later Babb's Secret Service supervisor phoned me and told me that Babbs was transferred to Washington, D.C., but he was calling me regarding my assisting them a month earlier.

He said, "Art, in appreciation for your assistance we have a potential informant for you if you are interested. We have a minor charge against him and will drop it if he agrees to help you. When we interrogated him, most of his information was drug trafficking-related."

"Sir, it would be my pleasure to take that guy off your hands."

The supervisor said, "Good. I made arrangements to have a meeting with the guy tomorrow at 10:00 a.m. here at our office. Is that convenient for you?"

"I will be there, sir, and thanks."

When I met the Secret Service supervisor and the potential informant named Benny (alias), the supervisor warned Benny, "Now remember, if you fail to help Agent Sedillo, we will file charges against you, and you will do time in federal prison. Do you understand?"

Benny answered, "Yes, sir. I swore that I would do the right thing, and thank you for letting me work off my beef."

I thanked the supervisor and walked out with my first informant. I brought Benny to my office and interviewed him. I laid out some basic ground rules of our relationship and assured him that I would do anything to help him if he was straight with me.

He said, "I know several pushers throughout the state. I did time in the joint with some of them who are now out and dealing shit."

We continued talking nonstop until three that afternoon. Benny has a photographic memory and kept identifying documented suspects throughout the state.

I prepared an organizational chart identifying the suspects and showed it to Lieutenant Sosa. He authorized me to launch a statewide undercover operation targeting the suspects identified.

Our first target was the Gomez brothers from Gallup, New Mexico. The suspects sold both heroin and marijuana. I had Benny make an undercover telephone call to them that on Friday evening we would be there to purchase two Prince Albert tobacco cans of marijuana.

On Friday afternoon we drove to Gallup and checked into a flea-bag motel and telephoned the suspects. They showed up, and after Benny introduced me as his brother-in-law, one of the suspects handed me the two cans of marijuana and I paid him forty dollars.

Three weeks later we took off to Roswell, New Mexico, and met with Agent James Sedillo. (Not related) James was glad to learn that Benny knew three of the Roswell major drug traffickers. We made plans to meet these suspects, and James assured us of his discreet surveillance to collaborate our contact with the suspects for our security. This was a refreshing experience since none of the other narcotics agents had offered to cover my ass.

We purchased marihuana and heroin from three suspects and subsequently they were arrested and prosecuted. Shortly after we made undercover drug purchases from suspects in Alamogordo and Las Cruces, New Mexico.

Lieutenant Sosa was most complimentary and gave me additional assignments. He told me that Silver City District Attorney David Serna had requested an undercover agent because of increased drug trafficking in Silver City and nearby Deming and Lordsburg, New Mexico.

To justify my extended time in Silver City, I was authorized to enroll in Western New Mexico University under my undercover name. Benny accompanied me.

A heavy snow welcomed us to this mountainous community. District Attorney Serna instructed me to drive to Sheriff Steven Aguirre's residence, where we enjoyed a work dinner.

During this meeting, District Attorney Serna briefed us on the suspects in his jurisdiction, and he was impressed to learn that Benny knew them. We were informed that the most dangerous of the suspects was Alberto Luna. Keeping this in mind, we worked out a plan to give the suspect the impression that we ran into him by accident, rather than going to his house directly.

District Attorney Serna set us up in a second-floor apartment in the downtown area. The following day I walked the short distance to the university and enrolled in a drama class.

On Saturday morning we conducted surveillance on Luna's house from a distance. After a couple of hours, we saw a black Chevy pickup arrive and park in front of his house. A tall and lanky guy in his thirties came out of the house and got into the truck.

Benny told me, "That's him."

We followed the truck to a nearby liquor store. Luna entered. We parked on the side and intentionally walked in bitching about the brand

DON'T EXPECT ANYTHING

of beer that we were going to buy. Luna overheard us and popped out of the second aisle and told Benny, "Benny, what the fuck? I knew that shitty voice of yours right away."

They hugged and laughed. Benny said, "What the hell are you doing in this shithole? I'm here with my brother-in-law who's attending college. I'm keeping an eye on him so that he doesn't mess around with the young chicks."

Luna said, "I live here, dumb ass, and the only shithole in the state is where you live in Albuquerque."

I stepped into their path and extended my hand and introduced myself. "*Hola,* I'm Arturo Chavez. And don't pay attention to Benny. He will probably drive me crazy before the semester is over."

We walked out together after each purchased a six-pack of beer. Luna told us, "Look, can you guys give me a ride? I'll get rid of my cousin. He too, like Benny, is a pain in the ass. And besides that, his truck is a piece of shit."

I said, "Sure man, today is Saturday, and I have no classes."

Luna told his cousin to leave, then jumped into the back of the car and said, "Man, your wheels are pretty good."

His next words floored us.

Luna said, "Listen, guys. I have to go to the Mexican border to pick up my bi-weekly order of *motá* (marijuana). Can you guys give me a ride there? I'll pay for your gas, and if you guys want some pot, I'll give you a hell of a deal."

Benny and I looked at each other in surprise that we had not said shit about drugs, and this idiot, the meanest and biggest doper in the area, just set himself up and fell into our hands.

I told him, "Look, man, I can't take my car to Mexico and take the chance of getting busted on our way back by the Border Patrol." I intentionally said Border Patrol to sound ignorant that it was U.S. Customs and not the Border Patrol that intercepts illicit drugs at the border.

Luna corrected me, saying, "The Border Patrol only busts 'wets,' man. You mean the U.S. Customs on the border. No dude, we don't cross the car. We park in the parking lot on the U.S. side and walk across the border."

"That I can do. No problem as long as I don't take my wheels to the other side."

"Like I said, no problem. We go to this bar right across the border, not more than a hundred yards. From there I go and talk to my man. They cross the shit for me, and we walk back. I pick it up on this side, and we are on our way home."

At his house, Luna excused himself for a short while. He came out wearing an ironed white long-sleeved shirt, Levis, and a light windbreaker jacket.

Luna talked all the damn way to the Arizona-Mexican border, telling stupid stories of shit they pulled in prison. Benny kept encouraging him, and in doing so, we learned of another ex-con they both knew who was dealing marijuana in Deming, New Mexico.

When we got to Douglas, Arizona, I parked the car at the stateside border parking lot, and the three of us walked across the border without incident. On the Mexican side we continued half a block to the canary-yellow-painted bar with a large coin shape of a silver dollar identifying the establishment as the Silver Dollar Bar.

Inside the décor was mostly American Western with wagon wheels and deer heads mounted on the walls. We sat at a corner table and ordered tacos and beer.

Before Luna left, I told him, "Look, man, as soon as Benny and I finish eating, we are going to walk back and wait for you in the car. Since you usually come alone, why do this differently and attract the attention of the damn Customs people?"

Luna stared at me for a while and then told Benny, "It's nice to have someone who is intelligent. I think that's a good idea. Just let me split for a short while before you leave."

A couple of minutes after Luna left, we paid the bill and walked back to the border, where I identified myself to the U.S. Customs

DON'T EXPECT ANYTHING

inspector and explained our situation, requesting his assistance in permitting us to pursue our investigation.

I provided him with Lieutenant Sosa's telephone number as well as the Silver City district attorney's number, so he could verify what I had told him.

At first he was a bit hesitant, perhaps trying to digest all I said. He then got on the telephone and talked to his supervisor. At the end of the call, he wished us luck and let us go.

Half an hour later Luna joined us with glassy eyes and laughing. He said, "Okay, guys, everything worked out perfect, now drive a couple of blocks the way we came, and I will tell you where to stop and wait for me."

I followed his instructions, and we dropped him off near the entrance to an alley, which he took and disappeared. About half an hour later he came back carrying a gunnysack full of marihuana.

We were glad that he was stoned, drunk, or both, because after he got into the backseat of the car, he fell asleep. Eventually, an hour or so later, we passed the Rodeo, New Mexico, village. Once I saw that we were back in New Mexico jurisdiction, my nerves settled.

When we arrived at Luna's house, he invited us in so he could weigh the kilogram of marijuana that he was going to sell us. I told him to forget about reimbursing me for the gas, since he had given us a hell of a good deal on the marijuana.

When we walked into his house, he proved to be a total scumbag. His two-year-old child was crawling on the kitchen floor, and Luna put his boot under him and kicked him through an open door into the other room as he yelled at his wife, "How many fucking times have I told you to keep the kids out of my way when I'm conducting business?"

His wife, with tears of hate, just stared at the three of us as she picked up the crying child and comforted him.

Luna weighed the kilogram of marijuana, put it in a brown paper bag, and gave it to me. I handed him fifty dollars. We thanked each other, agreeing to stay in touch for additional purchases.

Benny and I initiated additional cases on several other suspects in Silver City, Deming, and Lordsburg, New Mexico. To further implicate the suspects, I introduced them to NMSP Agents George Ulibarri and James Sedillo for additional undercover drug purchases.

Three weeks later on a Friday morning, we conducted a raid and arrested six suspects. Luna was found guilty and sentenced to life in prison for the habitual criminal acts since it would be his third time imprisoned.

Seeing the result, the other defendants entered a guilty plea, putting themselves at the mercy of the judge for reduced sentences.

Benny assisted me so much that District Attorney David Serna made an official petition to the New Mexico governor for his complete pardon, which was granted.

CHAPTER 11

SINCE I HAD not received any narcotics enforcement training, Captain T. J. Chavez selected me to attend a Federal Bureau of Narcotics (FBN) three-day seminar in Long Beach, California, with him.

At the Long Beach resort motel we joined several other state narcotics agents where FBN issued us name tags and instructed us to wear them at all conference functions. The opening ceremony was followed by Happy Hour.

Captain Chavez had told me, "Art, through the years I have learned that besides what you learn at these conferences, it is an opportunity to meet and befriend fellow agents from other states and in particular, neighboring states. This is important in the event you have to coordinate the location of fugitives that may have escaped to neighboring states. It makes it a lot easier to follow up on these types of investigation if you already know your neighboring counterparts."

"Yes, sir."

"Knock off the 'sir,' and to better make more contacts, we will socialize separately."

"Okay."

At the Happy Hour two Mexican Federal Judicial Police (MFJP) agents approached me and asked me if I spoke Spanish.

"Of course I do. Can I be of any service to you guys?"

They introduced themselves as Agents Ignacio Sanchez Nieda and Carlos Rodriguez Fitzgerald. Carlos said, "We speak some English, but not that well. Would you mind hanging out with us so you can translate for us if we get stuck?"

"Sure, it would be my pleasure. My name is Arturo Sedillo, and I'm a New Mexico State Police Narcotics Agent.

For the rest of the Happy Hour and the conference we were inseparable. Later on the other federal and state agents kept complimenting my English, thinking I belonged to the Mexican Federal Police. I got tired of correcting them and let them think whatever.

When we reported to the conference room we were glad that our last names followed each other alphabetically so we were able to sit together and I continued translating for them.

At the closing ceremony, FBN Commissioner Harry Giordano gave an outstanding speech highlighting the need for federal and state narcotics enforcement coordination. At his conclusion he asked if anyone had any questions. Needless to say that protocol prevented anyone from asking anything.

Unfortunately my new buddy, Agent Sanchez Nieda, told me, "Ask him why they don't open an FBN office at the Guadalajara, Mexico-U.S. Consulate."

I argued with him that we were not supposed to ask him any questions.

He told me, "Bullshit; he just asked if we had any questions, and my grandfather, who is in the Supreme Court, specifically asked me to ask that question."

We were drawing too much attention arguing, so I stood up and asked the commissioner, "Sir, why hasn't FBN opened an office at the Guadalajara, Mexico-U.S. Consulate?"

Immediately all the suits on the podium circled the commissioner

DON'T EXPECT ANYTHING

and Los Angeles, California, Regional Director Ben Theisen walked down toward us. He must have seen that our table name tags all included the word *Mexico* and disregarded the word *New* in front of mine. He returned to the podium and reported his finding to the commissioner, who in turn told me, "I would very much like to invite the three of you to my suite to talk about this in private."

The session was dismissed, and I quickly told Captain T. J. Chavez what was going on. He told me he would be waiting for me at our rooms. Theisen came for the three of us and escorted us to Commissioner Giordano's suite. We joined the commissioner and several members of his staff who quickly prepared us cocktails of our choices.

At that point I had come to the conclusion that they all thought I was a Mexican fed, which I found a bit humorous in the sense that they must have known that they had invited only two MFJP agents, so who in the hell else could I be? When I told them about the confusion and that I was a New Mexico State Police narcotics agent, everyone frowned until I qualified my remark that I had asked the question on behalf of MFJP Agent Sanchez, whose grandfather was in the Mexican Supreme Court and had asked Sanchez Nieda to ask this question.

Smiles popped all over.

Commissioner Giordano asked me to have Agent Sanchez tell his grandfather that he was very interested in opening an office in the U.S. Consulate at Guadalajara, Mexico, and would pursue that interest with the U.S. Department of State, the American ambassador in Mexico City, and the Mexican authorities. He added that having a BNDD office at the Guadalajara, Mexico-U.S. Consulate was a top priority.

MFJP Sanchez Nieda was pleased with the response and gave the commissioner his grandfather's business card. After we exchanged farewells, Commissioner Giordano walked with me a ways on the hallway and told me, "Agent Sedillo, I want you to know that I appreciate very much your assistance in this important diplomatic matter."

"Sir, it was my pleasure to assist." We shook hands and went our separate ways.

CHAPTER 11

Back in the motel rooms I explained to Captain Chavez what had taken place, and he gave me an "Atta boy."

Relocating from Los Padillas to downtown Albuquerque was a sad but necessary move. Number one, God was going to bless us with a fourth child, and we prayed that it would be a boy so that Andrew would have a buddy for life. Being closer to a hospital was a priority. Secondly, moving to Los Padillas was to better service those communities as a state police trooper. Since I was now a narcotics agent, that priority was no longer applicable.

On May 18, 1966, I had to testify in Roswell, and by all indications Gino was going to be born on that date. Lieutenant Sosa made arrangements for the NMSP aircraft to take me to and from Roswell. Unfortunately, after the plane dropped me off, it had to go to another location in response to an emergency.

As soon as I finished testifying, Lieutenant Sosa must have broken the speed record in rushing me back to Albuquerque, getting me there shortly after Mariana had a Caesarian birth for our son Gino. When I got to the hospital, I walked up and down the halls praying the rosary on my fingers that both Mariana and Gino would be okay. A week later Mariana and Gino were released. This birth was also one of the happiest days in my life. I was also able to rock Gino as I sang him the U.S. Marines hymn.

Two months later I was transferred to Las Cruces, New Mexico, as the narcotics agent in charge. This title was mostly symbolic in the sense that I still had no subordinates and my salary didn't change. Mariana was also transferred to the Las Cruces State Motor Vehicle Department.

During the first days, I maintained a low profile, meeting only District Attorney Ernie Williams, Chief of City Police Silva, and his detective, Guzman. Guzman could have easily passed as a double for movie actor Lou Chaney, Jr. He was an outstanding detective, and we were able to work on several bilateral cases.

In coordination with U.S. Customs, on several locations I assisted them working undercover where I would meet heroin traffickers at a Juarez, Mexico, hotel and make arrangements for them to deliver me the heroin purchased at El Paso, Texas. Of course those transactions never materialized because the Customs agents would arrest them at the international port of entry when they attempted to smuggle the heroin.

To further conceal my undercover status during my first days at Las Cruces, I enrolled in the university drama class and invited suspects to view my minor roles in some of the plays. At the end of this phase, we arrested six suspects.

During the prosecution of one of those defendants and while testifying against him, I noticed a man in the audience dressed in a suit and taking notes. I attempted to locate him after I testified, but he had left the courtroom. I continued to the district attorney's office and found the same person talking to the district attorney and a Hispanic secretary.

Upon seeing me, the district attorney introduced me to Leonardo Samudio and told me that he was the Chihuahua, Mexico, prosecuting attorney. Leonardo told me that in spite of his limited English, he was very interested in learning the American criminal justice process.

I took him to my office and briefed him in our criminal justice process. I invited him to join my family for supper, and by the end of the day we had become good friends. He invited me to Chihuahua so he could explain its judicial system.

After obtaining Chief Black's permission, I went to Chihuahua, and Leonardo gave me an excellent briefing on the Mexican state judicial process. We agreed to stay in touch and whenever possible coordinate bilateral investigations without compromising our respective federal jurisdictions.

Chapter 12

I'm not superstitious, but strangely enough, every year around my birthday, February 2, something positive happens in my life. For one, I married Mariana on my twenty-fifth birthday.

Well, a day after my thirtieth birthday, February 3, 1968, Albuquerque Federal Bureau of Narcotics Agent in Charge Johnny Thompson telephoned me, and after exchanging salutations, asked me, "Art, remember that FBN conference you attended some time ago at Long Beach, California?"

"I sure do. Enjoyed it very much."

"Well, remember you befriended two Mexican Federal Police, and on behalf of them you coordinated a meeting with National Commissioner Harry Giordano for preliminary diplomatic negotiations to open an office at our U.S. Consulate in Guadalajara, Mexico?"

"Yes, sir."

"Good. I may have some good news for you. Commissioner Giordano was most impressed with you and requested that we ask you if you would be interested in becoming a Federal Bureau of Narcotics agent."

I was speechless for a short while and then responded, "Sir, please tell Commissioner Giordano that it would be an honor and pleasure to be considered for such a position."

"Great, please consider this offer confidential for the time being. I would like to go down there to Las Cruces this Friday to initiate the hiring paperwork. Once we do it, you can notify your people and submit your resignation. How soon do you think you would be available?"

"As soon as we hang up."

We laughed. He agreed to come down on Friday. I told him to come with a good appetite, because Mariana and I would take him to eat at the famous Maria's restaurant in Juarez, Mexico.

After hanging up the phone, Mariana, who was preparing supper, asked me, "What's up?"

I hugged her and said, "The Federal Bureau of Narcotics just offered me a job as a FBN agent." She joined my excitement, knowing that it had been my unforeseeable goal. I told her, "Honey, I feel like a kid who was kicking a football in our backyard and from there I got drafted into the NFL."

Agent Thompson arrived that Friday afternoon, and we took care of the administrative paperwork to get me processed into the FBN. He told me, "We already finished your background investigation for clearance into the agency, and all we need to process is these two final forms that need your signature."

After we completed the paperwork, Mariana joined us, and we drove to Juarez to eat at Maria's. After an excellent supper, we enjoyed a couple of margaritas and listened to the mariachis perform. After this mini celebration, Mariana drove us back to Las Cruces.

On March 25, Agent Thompson telephoned me. "Art, congratulations and welcome aboard. You have now been officially accepted by FBN. You can now submit your resignation to the state police."

"Thank you, sir, I will take care of that immediately."

He told me, "Your reporting date to our Denver, Colorado, regional office is April 1. I want you to stop at our office when you are on your way to Denver so we can swear you in."

"Yes, sir."

After receiving this good news, Mariana and I drafted our letters of resignation to the State Police and the Motor Vehicle Department.

On Monday, April 1, 1968, my departure was most emotional, because I realized it was not a normal going-out-of-town gig. Unable to restrain our tears, I kissed Mariana and the kids and headed north. Mariana and the kids would follow after the end of the school year, in June.

I stopped at the FBN office at Albuquerque, and after a fast ceremonial swearing in, Agent Thompson told me, "Art, you may not realize the history you have already created in our agency. For your information, you are the last FBN agent hired in our organization. Next week, by presidential mandate, President Nixon will abolish FBN, and our organization will be transferred from the U.S. Treasury Department to the U.S. Department of Justice under our new title of Bureau of Narcotics and Dangerous Drugs (BNDD). He issued me the last FBN badge.

When I arrived at the Denver, Colorado, federal building I found the FBN/BNDD office in a shadowy basement corner. I knocked on the door, and a chubby, thirtyish, balding guy opened the door and asked me in an unfriendly manner, "Yeah, what do you want?"

I said, "My name is Arthur Sedillo, and I was instructed by Agent Johnny Thompson to report to work here."

The transformation of the guy was immediate. He broke out in a big smile and extended a handshake. "Oh, that's right. We were expecting you. I'm Bob Wilkins. Come right in." He escorted me to Regional Director William Wanzeck's office.

Before I entered the regional director's office, a second agent named John Zienter greeted me with a friendly hand wave. Besides these two agents and the regional director, a woman in her mid-forties named Naomi was the office secretary. Regional Director Wanzeck's area of responsibility includes the states of Colorado, Wyoming, New Mexico, and Utah.

After exchanging greetings, Regional Director Wanzeck told me, "Since you were hired under unusual circumstances, it is imperative that you familiarize yourself with our enforcement and administrative manuals. A basic training seminar is not scheduled until much later on, so you will have to learn this stuff on your own. Our personnel is available to assist you, but I don't expect you to become their burden. Do you understand?"

"Yes, sir."

"After you finish studying the manuals and reviewing case files, report back to me for additional instructions. Take a couple of weeks to do it. Do you have any questions?"

"Only one, sir. Would it be okay for me to return my car to my family on the weekend? I'll come right back on the bus."

"No problem. Have Naomi provide you with the manuals and take care of other pending administrative matters."

During lunch, Bob and John invited me to accompany them to the cafeteria on the basement level, where they introduced me to U.S. Customs Agent Bob King. Bob told me, "Our agents in El Paso, Texas, told me you would be joining these losers instead of joining us. They told me you had helped them on many cases and I should help you whenever possible."

"Thanks, Bob. Yes, I had lots of fun posing as doper and meeting heroin pushers at a Juarez, Mexico, hotel and setting them up to deliver me heroin at El Paso. But of course the delivery never happened, because your people busted them at the port of entry."

For the rest of the day and the following two weeks, I studied the manuals and investigative files. I did return the car to Mariana and the kids and enjoyed a short visit before returning to Denver.

Back on the job I reported to Regional Director Wanzeck, telling him that I had finished reviewing the manuals and case files. After I answered several questions to his satisfaction, I was shocked with his following order. He told me, "Okay, Art, I heard you were a hell of a good undercover agent. I'm going to give you an opportunity to prove it. I want you to go out there and buy some dope, and don't come back until you have accomplished this mission."

He handed me a hundred dollars and wished me luck. I was not furnished a car, informant, or back up agents. I couldn't believe that he was sending me out alone just like that.

After getting over the shock, I hit the Denver Streets, and to further piss me off, it was April, and instead of being able to enjoy the Las Cruces April showers, I found myself walking in snow in Denver.

I hopped on a municipal transit bus traveling toward Federal and 28th streets. In reviewing some general files, I learned that some heroin traffickers patronized a bar in that general area.

When I reached the area, I noticed that two bars faced each other separated by 35th Street. Shivering, I walked into the nicer one and sat on a corner stool near a potbelly heater. "What the hell is this, snow falling in April?" I asked the friendly bartender.

He told me, "Obviously you are not from here. It is not unusual for snow to start falling in April."

I ordered a beer and two tacos after smelling the rich chili aroma coming from the mini kitchen at the end of the bar. The bartender, who appeared to be in his mid-thirties, was the owner. His wife was the cook and worked the cash register.

I heard them complaining as they looked out the window and saw people parking their cars in their parking lot and patronizing the bar across the street. Taking advantage of this situation, I interrupted them, saying, "Pardon me for eavesdropping, but I may be able to solve your problem. I'm a sign painter and can make you a sign with the wording 'Parking for Customers Only; Others Will Be Towed at Owner's Expense' or something like that."

The wife answered me, "That sounds great. How much would you charge us?"

"Let's go outside so I can get the measurements."

The owner, who introduced himself as John, accompanied me, and I made some mental calculations and told him that the sign would be two and a half by four feet. The letters would be red on a white background. The owners agreed, and I told them that it would cost $20.00, but instead of paying me cash, to give me a $20.00 tab at the bar, since I planned to patronize it more often. They agreed.

What gave me the sign idea is that when I was getting on the bus, I noticed a sign shop specializing in small and big signs.

On my way to my apartment I got off the bus near the sign shop. I knocked on the door, and an elderly man asked me, "What do you want?" His tone sounded as if he was pissed.

I told him, "I came to buy a loaf of bread."

This response kind of broke his shitty spell, and he asked me, "Are you a clown or what?"

I told him I needed a small sign, and he waved me into his shop. I explained what I needed, and he told me that he was now in a good mood and would charge me only $15.00 for the sign and it would be ready the following morning. He was drinking Mogen David wine and filled a second glass for me. We chitchatted for a while and I agreed to pick up the sign the following morning.

The following day I picked up the sign and a few nails and boarded the bus to 35th Street. Because of the blizzard-like weather, I used the sign to cover my head and better navigate through the storm.

I had telephoned John to make sure he would be at the bar that early in the morning. When I got there, I lied to him that my partner had dropped me off, because he had to go to another job. He provided me with a ladder and a hammer. I nailed up the sign, and the owners liked it.

On Monday afternoon I returned to the bar, and John told me, "Arturo, your sign works. Already a guy was going to park, but kept going after seeing the sign."

I ordered a beer and a taco and noticed four possible suspects at a corner table. They appeared to be arguing about the price of whatever they were buying.

A Chicano about twenty-five years old and a bit on the heavy side

CHAPTER 12

sat next to me at the counter. I asked him in Spanish if he had a match to light my cigarette. He responded in a loud voice, "Look, you, we speak the English here in America."

I responded as loud in English, "Forgive me for offending you. It's that you look more Mexican then Pancho Villa, and your English sucks. If you're going to criticize anyone, the least you could do is speak correctly, you dumb ass."

His reaction was what I expected. He stood up and threw wild haymaker punches, missing me as I ducked them. I counterpunched and dumped him on the floor.

By then John, the bar owner, came around and told the guy to get the hell out of his bar and not return. As the guy walked out of the bar, I noticed the suspects at the corner table clap their hands and give me a thumbs up.

Shortly afterward all the suspects but one left, and the remaining guy came and sat by me. He introduced himself as Julio, and I told him I was Arturo Chavez.

He told me, "That *pendejo* you punched out is a troublemaker, and we were sure glad you cleaned his clock."

I ordered both of us another beer and told John to put it on my tab, making sure that Julio heard me. We continued talking about the Denver Broncos football team and the shitty weather.

After feeling more confident, I told Julio, "Look, man, it is none of my business, but you should be more careful. I could hear you guys arguing about the price for *chiva* (heroin), and that guy I punched out kept trying to overhear your conversation. He may have been a snitch or something like that."

Julio said, "You are so right. Sometimes I get pissed and raise my voice. It's that these guys think I'm Santa Claus and want to give away my stuff for nothing."

I intentionally changed the subject and started talking about Martin Luther King's recent assassination and other current news media.

Julio said, "Shit, I better call it a day. I sold all my shit with the

DON'T EXPECT ANYTHING

exception of two tins."

I could not believe the idiot was so open about it. Acting dumb, I asked, "Two tins of what, *chiva* or pot?"

He told me, "*Chiva*. Would you be interested in buying them? I sell them at ten dollars each, but I'll sell them both to you for ten bucks."

I told him, "You know what? I don't shoot up, but I have this girlfriend that pops every once in a long while. Maybe if I take her some she will treat me fine. Yeah, what the hell, here are the ten bucks."

Julio handed me the two heroin tins, and before he departed, we agreed to stay in touch.

It should be noted that neither bar owners John or his wife were involved in the drug business. Actually Julio told me he liked to do business at that location because it was clean and didn't attract the police.

CHAPTER 13

THE DAY THAT I turned in my heroin purchase, the boss issued me an official government vehicle (OGV), a gas credit card, a snub-nosed 38-caliber pistol, and other official goodies. During this mini-presentation I was issued my new U.S. Justice Department Bureau of Narcotics and Dangerous Drugs (BNDD) badge. I was permitted to keep my FBN badge as a historical memento as the last one issued.

Sometime afterward, I picked up my family from Las Cruces. We rented a three-bedroom house in Northglenn, a Denver suburb. Right away Mariana obtained a job at Northglenn Dodge Dealership as an administrative assistant.

The house we rented was in a nice middle-class neighborhood. We noticed that our Hispanic next-door neighbors did not appear to be friendly, and then on an early morning, I arrived home from an overnight surveillance and saw for the first time my neighbor came out of his house dressed in a Denver police officer's uniform.

I walked up to him and introduced myself, flashing him with my BNDD badge. He broke out in a big smile and friendly handshake and introduced himself as Frank Rivera. He said, "Well, I'll be damned, neighbor, when you guys first moved here and I noticed you coming home at weird hours in different cars, I thought for sure you were some king of thug. No wonder I was not able to get your vehicle license plate information."

I kidded with him, saying, "I thought that you guys were just uppity unfriendly Chicanos." We laughed, and at that very moment went for our wives and introduced them to each other. We became best of friends, and I felt more secure for my family having one of Denver's finest next door.

At work Mrs. Naomi told me, "Art, we have a walk-in informant that wants to talk to you."

My first impression was that my fellow agents were dumping me the "walk-in" snitch. That type of informant is usually questionable or could be a punk the criminal element sent to identify the agents.

I walked to the waiting room and found a short, thin guy in his mid-forties dressed in a white baker's outfit with a doughnut logo above the shirt pocket. Upon seeing me he said, "You must be Agent Sedillo."

I asked him, "And how do you know that?"

He said, "Those other two guys are crackers like me, right?"

"Can't argue with that logic. How did you know about me?"

He said, "I'll tell you all you want to know, but let's back up a bit. I want to apologize for showing up in my work clothes, but this was the only time I had to come here. I work in a doughnut shop."

He continued, "Now regarding your question of how I know about you, U.S. Customs Agent King referred me to you. You can check with him to see that I'm not shitting you.

"I consider Agent King a good friend, and if he referred you to me, it was with good intentions. How can I help you?"

"Don't laugh, but my name is Johnny Dough, you know how you Feds call someone you don't know 'John Doe.' Well, I'm for real. As to your question, it's a matter of helping you and maybe as a result of that, I will benefit from it also."

I walked Johnny to my desk and got us cups of coffee. Johnny said,

"Most of my life I have been a dope-head. I lost my wife and two kids and spent most of my adult life doing time in the slammer or shooting shit up my veins. I have come to the conclusion that the only way to get serious about this is by burning these dopers that helped me become a junkie. I know one of the principle heroin sources of supply in Colorado and can help you bust his ass."

"Congratulations for making this decision in your life. Identify this guy, name, physical description, and so forth, so I can check to see if we have him in our files."

"You must have something on him, because he did time in prison when he lived in New Orleans, but now he resides here in Denver. His name is Bruce Cunningham (alias), about thirty-two years old, heavy-set but sloppy build.

"The guy delivers shit to me at the doughnut shop early on Sunday mornings. He knows you guys are not working on Sundays and definitely not that early in the mornings."

"I hate to admit it, but the guy is probably right."

"Look, Art, I work in the doughnut shop from four in the morning to noon. If you could be working with me, I could tell Bruce that we are buddies so that eventually he will agree to sell you dope."

"Johnny, let me run this down to my boss, which I'm sure he will approve. But look, better than to say that we are buddies, let's tell him we are brothers-in-law or that I'm married to your first cousin or something like that."

"Shit, you will not believe it, but I have a cousin that is married to a Chicano and they live in Albuquerque, New Mexico."

"That is great, I'm from New Mexico too. What about your doughnut shop boss? Will he be pissed seeing me there?"

"Hell no. He knows I need help, and I will bullshit him that you will be helping me for free and that if you work out good, he may want to hire you."

I processed Johnny as my first Federal cooperating individual (CI). Before he departed, he told me about a Salvation Army retail shop where I would be able to purchase a cheap baker's outfit.

The following morning at the ungodly hour of 3:00 a.m., I picked up Johnny and we went to the doughnut shop. Johnny got a pot of coffee going and he started teaching me how to make doughnuts.

Two days later we heard a loud knock on the rear door, and Johnny told me, "That's him." He opened the door and told Bruce, "Hey, bro, I thought you'd bought the farm or split from the scene. Where in the hell have you been?"

Bruce told him, "Fuck you, dumb ass. You are eating too many doughnuts, and they are starting to damage your little brain. Don't you remember that I told you I would be out of town until today, Thursday?"

Johnny told him that he had forgotten and turned around and told me, "Arturo, come. I want to introduce you to this guy, and bring four dozen doughnuts that we will pack for him." He then told Bruce, "Arturo is my sister's brother-in-law and will be working with me for a while."

Bruce greeted me in a friendly manner as Johnny started packing the doughnuts in a large brown bag. He had told me that each time Bruce came, he bought four dozen. Johnny also put the money in the doughnut sack for the heroin he was purchasing from Bruce, which was usually four tin-foil packets of heroin for forty dollars.

After packing the doughnuts, Johnny made a funny face and told Bruce, "Man, I have to take a shit real bad. Arturo will bring you the doughnuts. Give him the four tins. The cash is in the bag."

I had previously briefed Johnny that as soon as possible, we should negotiate with Bruce in a manner that I got involved in the actual drug and money transaction. The scam that he pulled about having to take a dump worked out perfectly.

I followed Bruce to his 1966 Cadillac and handed him the bag with the doughnuts and told him, "The forty bucks are in the small plastic bag."

He said, "Okay" as he bent over a bit and took out a leather bank bag, unzipped it, and took out four tin-foil packets containing heroin and handed them to me.

He said, "Tell Johnny I'll be back next week at the same time."

"Got you."

I was glad for making the direct transaction case, but also relieved that I would not have to get up at three in the morning until the following Sunday. Another good thing was that when we arrested Bruce, his beautiful Caddy would become ours, since he used it in transporting illicit narcotics.

Of course my fellow agents were not happy having to get up early the following Sunday to conduct surveillance on my follow-up heroin purchase.

After the second buy, I told Bruce, "Look, man, I'm not an early person, and this working at the doughnut shop sucks. I know that you don't like doing business during regular hours, but next week I'm taking some pot to clients in Wyoming, and they have asked for five tins of heroin. I will be taking off for over there at about seven at night. Would it be possible for you to sell me the tins at about six that Friday evening?"

He said, "No fucking way."

I told him, "No problem. I have another source; I just wanted to give you the business."

He hesitated a while and then said, "Okay, I'll do it this time."

He gave me his telephone number and home address and said, "Be sure and don't make it later than six, because I hit the sack early, and I'm a light sleeper."

"You got it, my man."

The following Friday I drove to his house, and after the third series of door knocks and no answer, I sat on the porch swing and kept calling Bruce's name.

Finally he came out dressed in blue silk pajamas.

"Shit," I told him, "You were not kidding that you are an early bird in hitting the sack."

DON'T EXPECT ANYTHING

He was in a shitty mood and told me, "Here is your stuff. Give me my money and get the hell out of my sight."

I discreetly gave the surveillance team a thumbs up, letting them know they could go home. Agent Zienter accompanied me to the office to process the evidence. On Monday I mailed the evidence to our headquarters lab.

A couple of weeks later, on a heavily raining day, I telephoned Bruce to buy four more heroin tin-foil packets. I showed up at his house wearing my London Fog raincoat and fedora. When I knocked on his door, I decided to joke with him and said, "It's the FBI, fucker. Open the door."

I heard some rumbling and a toilet flushing, and then he opened the door scared shitless. Upon seeing that it was me, he got all pissed off and told me, "You dumb piece of shit. Now you will have to pay me for the stuff that I flushed. That was ten tin foils, so that's a hundred bucks."

I could hear a female laughing inside the house, and she must have heard me also. I told Bruce, "Sorry, man, now I know that was not a very good prank to pull on you. Look, I have the forty dollars for the four tin foils, but I promise you that next week I'll buy four more and bring you the extra hundred, okay?"

"Okay, sit your ass on the swing. I have to go to my car." He went back into the house and on to the garage behind the house. Shortly afterward he returned and handed me the tin foils in exchange for the forty dollars.

On the following Friday late afternoon, we set up a raiding party involving three other agents. Two approached the house from the rear garage entrance and two of us through the front door. I knocked on the door and announced, "Open the door. This is the Bureau of Narcotics and Dangerous Drugs."

Bruce responded, "Shut the fuck up, Art. The first time it was funny, but you're starting to piss me off." At that point he opened the door and saw the two of us pointing our pistols at him.

He dropped the heroin baggy and almost crying begged us, "Please, guys, don't hurt me. Here, you can take this free of charge. Please don't hurt me." By then the rest of the team was inside the house, and they seized the additional heroin tins that were on the table. They also seized his Cadillac.

We put him in the back seat of my car. As we drove off, he was still under the impression that we were thugs who had just ripped him off and were probably going to kill him. When he saw us drive into the Federal Building basement parking, he was overjoyed and said, "Oh, my God. Thank God you guys are for real."

He did not hesitate to identify his source of heroin supply, who was subsequently indicted. Because of his cooperation, his sentence was reduced.

CHAPTER 14

ON A COLD winter Friday morning, our U.S. assistant attorney, a young gong-ho black prosecuting attorney, called me to his office and referred me to a black community leader I will call Mr. Daniels.

I drove to Mr. Daniels's residence located in an affluent area. He was standing by for me and guided me into his third car garage space.

After exchanging greetings, I followed him into his comfortable den. The fireplace was ignited and the view through his bay window of large snowflakes falling on the tall pine trees made the scene perfect for a Christmas card. Mrs. Daniels served us hot chocolate and then excused herself so we could talk.

Mr. Daniels said, "Art, first, thanks for your quick response. The U.S. attorney and I are old good friends, and I'm also grateful to him for getting us together."

"Sir, the pleasure is mine. How can I help you?"

"We have a drug trafficker named Clarence Jones who is providing cocaine to our younger kids, and we have come up with a possible plan to immobilize him. This is where we need you, but let me give you more details to see if you think our plan is feasible."

"Yes, sir."

"We have a person who was close to Clarence, but even he is down on him, because Clarence gave his young daughter some cocaine and she almost overdosed and had to be hospitalized."

"What an idiot! These are the suspects that I love to bust."

"He is more than an idiot. He is a child molester. Anyway, our contact can set up Clarence with a telephone call to sell you cocaine."

"How can he do that?"

"Our source has assured me that he can call Clarence and tell him to deliver cocaine to any client. The only thing that Clarence has requested is to make the transaction on a Sunday because he feels you narcos will not be working on Sunday mornings.

"I recently worked another case that the doper had the same criteria. These traffickers must talk to each other."

"Art, my man says it will be that simple. All we have to do is select some location, preferably on the southwest side of town. We set up a time and place and how much you want to buy. He sells the cocaine capsules for ten dollars each. All I need to complete this proposed transaction is your undercover name."

"Good, tell your source that we will buy ten capsules for a hundred dollars and my name will be Arturo Chavez. When I was coming over here I noticed a Safeway store about half a mile from here, and it has a large parking lot. How would that work out for Clarence? Another Hispanic agent will be with me, since too much surveillance may spook Clarence."

"That's a good idea, but can you call me later this evening to confirm the meeting? Just let me tell you one more thing. Our source said that once Clarence learns that he sold drugs to a federal agent, he will probably cop to a guilty plea, hoping to get a reduced sentence."

"Mr. Daniels, here is my business card with my home phone number on the back. Feel free to call me whenever you need me. I will call you to confirm the transaction."

At the office I called Agent Chris Saiz to come to my cubicle to finalize our undercover plan. I told him, "This Sunday you and I will be working undercover and making history. As you know, no one has made an undercover purchase of cocaine in this state, so stick around with me, and I'll make you famous."

Chris said, "You are full of shit. Virgie and I have plans to play tennis on Sunday, so I will not be available."

"Bullshit. Besides, it is going to be snowing, and you will not be able to see the white tennis balls. People seeing you play will only bring embarrassment to all of us Hispanics."

"We are playing indoors, shit for brains."

Agent Saiz and his wife Virgie had become dear friends of Mariana's and mine. They were also from New Mexico. Agent Saiz was a former FBN agent but had gone with BDAC (Bureau of Drug Abuse Control) and was now back with us as a result of the BNDD reorganization.

His giving me a hard time was playful, since he was as excited as I was to be the first agents to make an undercover purchase of cocaine in the state of Colorado.

On Sunday morning I picked up Agent Saiz and we drove slowly in the blizzard. We reached the five-point Safeway and parked in the middle of the empty parking lot.

Chris kept bitching that no sane person would be out in this storm. While he bitched, a black guy walked up to our car, and we played the role of ignoring him and kept bitching at each other. After the third set of knocks on the window, I lowered the window and said, "Yeah, what the hell do you want?"

Clarence said, "Fuck you, man. I thought you were somebody else."

As he started to walk off, I asked him, "Are you Clarence?"

He smiled and walked back and asked, "Are you Arturo Chavez?"

"Yeah, man. Here, get into the backseat before you freeze your balls."

He got into the back, and I asked him, "Do you have my ten things?"

He opened his winter parka and handed me ten capsules of cocaine in a small plastic bag. I gave him five twenty-dollar bills.

CHAPTER 14

I told him, "Look, man, it is none of my business how you work, but I prefer to keep it to a minimum of persons involved. Since we now know each other, why bother with a go-between that got us together this time? You will not have to pay him a commission or whatever; besides that, the fewer people involved, the better."

He agreed and asked me for a pen or pencil to write his telephone number.

I handed him my pen and he wrote his number on a piece of cardboard he tore off an empty beer container I had left in the backseat. He told me to call him whenever I needed more but said it would have to be a Sunday as the delivery day.

After he left, Chris and I gave each other a high five for making the first undercover cocaine case in the state. He then started chewing me out for giving Clarence my black U.S. Government ballpoint pen to write his telephone number. He said, "Good thing he is as dumb as you and he didn't snap on the U.S. Government pen."

Sometime after a couple more cocaine purchases from Clarence, he was arrested and prosecuted.

Later Chris was promoted to special agent in charge of the Salt Lake City, Utah, Office. Mariana and I would miss him and Virgie, but I couldn't resist harassing him for the last time, telling him that the Mormons didn't even smoke, so he would probably spend the majority of his time over there with his finger up his ass.

Unfortunately sometime afterward, Agent Saiz was wrongly implicated in a drug case in which the suspect claimed that the agent had planted the heroin on him. Chris was fired. After several months of litigation, he was completely exonerated of any wrongdoing.

When he was completely cleared, he had been working in a pharmacy in Salt Lake City. To celebrate, he and Virgie decided to have a party at their residence. While preparing for the party, Virgie went to the grocery store. While en route she was involved in an accident and was killed. When my wife and I heard about this tragedy, we were shocked and kept them both in our prayers.

CHAPTER 15

WHEN I RETURNED to work after two weeks of Christmas vacation, most of the agents were uptight after learning that the Headquarters Inspection Team had arrived unannounced. I was not concerned, remembering the previous year while we were still FBN agents, our office inspection consisted of elderly supervisory Agent Wayland Speer. When he arrived, Regional Director Wanzeck assigned me to pick up the inspector at the airport and transport him from the hotel to our office and to wherever he decided to go. I passed his inspection without any problems.

I got my cup of coffee and went to my cubbyhole to work, when to my surprise, midlevel supervisor Billy Ashcraft, also known to us agents as "Billy Blue," came to my desk accompanied by one of the inspectors and in a threatening manner said, "Drop whatever the hell you are working on and come to the chief inspector's office."

Knowing Billy Blue's profile, I was still not too concerned, but wondered what violation I was going to be accused of. Agent Ashcraft had the reputation of spending the majority of his time looking for agent's petty violations so he could write them up. For example, he would come to work earlier than anyone else and sneak to the basement parking area to see if an agent parked on an area not designated for agent parking or even if the agent parked over the yellow division parking space lines. He would write up the violator on blue paper, thus his alias of "Billy Blue."

I followed "Billy Blue" and the inspector to the conference room where the chief inspector and his two-man crew were conducting their inspection. "Billy Blue" attempted to sit down, but the chief inspector told him to get out. I smiled at him, further pissing him off.

The chief inspector instructed me to sit in front of his massive desk. I noticed one of my files on the desk, and the inspector asked me if I was familiar with that case.

I told him. "Yes, sir. What is the problem with it?"

He told me, "It has been brought to our attention that you withdrew three hundred dollars from the financial officer to make a drug buy, but the file reflects only two hundred dollars used. What happened to the other hundred dollars?"

"Sir, I can quickly explain that, but to do so, I will have to show you the case file I initiated after this one. Can I go get the file?"

He had one of his inspectors accompany me to the file room, where I checked out the file in question and handed it to the chief inspector. I pointed out where the hundred dollars in question had been applied to the purchase of drugs in the other case. Upon doing this, I said, "I'm sure that Supervisor Ashcraft brought this discrepancy to your attention, but if he had asked me about it, I would have explained it to him instead of wasting your time and mine.

"I would like to add one more thing. When the bureau gets good and ready to send me to its basic training session, I will document my investigative files as required. I have been writing them up the way I did in the New Mexico State Police Narcotics Unit in which once I withdrew money, I could apply it to several cases."

The chief inspector and his assistants agreed and dismissed me with smiles and handshakes. I was glad to see them pull "Billy Blue" into their office and obviously chew his ass out, because when they released him, he stormed out of the office with a flushed face.

In August 1969, I was finally sent to the BNDD Basic Training Course at our Washington, D.C., headquarters at the corner of 14th and I streets.

The first-floor entrance opened to a hallway leading to several commercial outlets including the Eagle Bar. Our class, which uniquely had several previous law enforcement guys, made this bar our hangout until the management complained to our headquarters, which in turn made the place off limits to us.

Our hotel was four blocks up 14th Street. My roommate, Agent Christopher Egan from Boston, and I found an Irish Pub around the corner and joined the local clients singing Irish songs.

We all kicked ass in the classroom, firearms, and physical training. Upon graduating, most of us received our new assignments. I was transferred to Dallas, Texas, and received my GS-9 promotion.

Back in Denver, after exchanging farewells with our dear neighbor friends Frank Rivera and family, we departed for Dallas, Texas, where we found a nice house in the Farmers' Branch suburb. After getting the kids enrolled in school, Mariana quickly got a job at a local Chrysler dealership.

On our first day reporting to work, Mariana drove me to the Federal Building, and I told her not to worry coming for me, since I would be getting a government vehicle. I reported to Regional Director Karadimas, who gave me a preliminary briefing and then assigned me to a group supervised by Agent Brown.

Group Supervisor Brown ordered me to travel to a ranch beyond the city limits to locate and arrest a BNDD fugitive. No one was assigned to assist me, which I found most unusual.

The actionable intelligence regarding the fugitive had to be worked right away, so I took off on my own, figuring the least I could do was find the fugitive's location to see if he was still there.

I stopped at a gas station in the general area near the fugitive's ranch. While the vehicle was being serviced, the proprietor heard a radio call coming from my car and asked me if I was some kind of law enforcement person. I identified myself and asked him if he knew the fugitive I was looking for and if he could give me directions to his ranch. He gave me the information requested. I thanked him and drove off.

Shortly afterward, as I was driving on a dirt road, I heard a loud truck horn as a truck drove parallel to me, and I noticed that the gas station owner was waving me to stop. He was accompanied by two other men.

He told me that he and his friends were honorary deputy sheriffs, and he had called the sheriff and obtained permission to help me locate and arrest the fugitive. One of the posse guys joined me in my car, and we followed the truck to the fugitive's ranch.

The fugitive was sitting in the front of his porch, and upon seeing us approaching him with weapons drawn, he responded, "What the hell is this?"

I identified myself as a BNDD agent and told him he was being arrested on drug and fugitive charges.

He calmed down and raised his hands, and we handcuffed him and placed him in the backseat of my unit. One of the deputies told me that he would accompany me to the Dallas jail. He said we would be doing each other a favor because he had to go to Dallas to pick up his truck that was being serviced there.

I thanked the other deputies, and on our way to Dallas stopped at a fast-food place and ordered jumbo cheeseburgers and a malt for each of us, knowing that by the time we got to jail, it would be after suppertime. The fugitive actually turned out to be a nice person, in spite of his notorious reputation.

The following morning back in the office I reported to Group Supervisor Brown that the fugitive was incarcerated and added that a sheriff's posse had assisted me.

On January 4, 1970, my new group supervisor, Agent Jesse Bautista,

DON'T EXPECT ANYTHING

stopped me as I entered our office after my Christmas vacation and told me, "Sedillo, report to the boss immediately." He pointed toward the director's office and added, "*Adios, amigo.*"

Regional Director Karadimas told me, "Art, headquarters has selected twelve agents to go on a very important assignment in Miami, Florida. Your selection was based on your Spanish-speaking and undercover abilities. This six months' assignment will spearhead a national and international investigation targeting the major Cuban-American drug trafficking organizations.

"This assignment is a definite plus in your career development in the sense that if it has positive results, your promotion and choice of duty reassignment is a sure thing."

"Thank you, sir. When will I be going?"

"Here is a copy of the telex. You can read it and then return it to the administrative officer to cut your orders and travel advance. Since they need you there next Monday, as soon as you finish any pending administrative work, take off the rest of the week on administrative leave."

I telephoned Mariana at her work. "Honey, I have some good and bad news, and if you can take an early break for lunch, an agent is dropping me off at your office in about an hour so I can tell you all about it."

Mariana responded, "Wait like hell. Tell me right now. What's up?"

I told her, "I have the rest of the week off. I have been assigned to a Miami, Florida, special task force. After this assignment the possibilities exist that I will be promoted and will have my choice of duty assignment."

She joyfully responded. "Wow, that is great, but what is the bad news?"

"The assignment is for a few months."

She said, "Oh, you're right. Hurry up so you can give me all the details. Okay?"

"I'm on my way."

Mariana got the rest of the day off, and we went to eat at an Italian restaurant. When we got home, we gave the kids a watered-down version of my assignment.

On January 10, 1970, I was on my way to Miami. At the Miami airport, I noticed the majority of the passengers and locals speaking Spanish with different accents, making me think that I had arrived in a Latin American country.

I took a taxi to the Center House Condominiums where the agents would be staying. The front-desk person gave me an envelope with the key to my condominium. I phoned Agent Hector Jordan, our task force supervisor, and he told me that a second Hispanic Texan named Ruben Monzon would be joining me. He told me that once he arrived we should go eat at the Cuban restaurant a block from the condos. He added that we should hit the sack early because we would be meeting in the lobby at five in the morning.

Shortly afterward Agent Monzon, a young, sharp-dressed guy, tie and all, arrived. I kidded him that I thought he was a Mormon wanting to convert me. He smiled and threw me the middle finger, blowing away the sanctimonious image I had mentioned.

We grabbed a Cuban sandwich and a beer at the nearby café and then hit the sack. At 5:OO a.m. the ten of us TDY agents met at the lobby and were escorted by two local agents to the Miami BNDD Office. I had befriended one of them, Agent Octavio Gonzalez, at our basic training session. We were taken to the Miami BNDD office through the rear entrance, because intelligence reflected that the traffickers were constantly conducting surveillance on the office to identify the agents.

At the office we hit the coffee and doughnut table and then sat as the "suits" (DEA headquarters bureaucrats), led by Agent Andy Tartaglino and Miami Regional Director Bernard Theisen, briefed us on the Cuban American cocaine trafficking organization operating out of the Miami, Florida, with connections to several metropolitan areas throughout the United States. The operation was named Operation Eagle.

Regional Director Theisen said, "You will operate a telephone wire-tap out of a safe house near the major violator's condominium. You will work, eat, and sleep on twenty-four shifts.

The supervisors continued explaining the logistics and tactical operations involved. An intelligence session followed with photos and videotapes.

After the session, we broke into teams and initiated surveillance of selected major violators. Each midnight after a twelve-hour workday we met at Group Supervisor Jordan's condo suite to recap our day's activities and get assignments for the following day.

Group Supervisor Hector Jordan was a tall Chicano in his mid-thirties with a light complexion, neck-length black hair, and a goatee. His angular face with deep-set eyes complimented his shitty smile that was misleading in the sense that one can't tell if he was content or pissed. We all respected him because of his undercover reputation.

After we spent a week on familiarization surveillance, our first task force assignments were made. Agents Jeff Hall, Gordon Rayner, Octavio Gonzales, and I were assigned to conduct surveillance on a major target's apartment. I teamed up with Agent Gonzales, and the four of us proceeded to our assignment.

Agent Gonzales told me to be cool and disregard the other team members, who were rushing to get the better surveillance location. Octavio told me, "We already have the best location."

The suspect's location reminded me of the *West Side Story* movie. Both sides of the block had four-story brick apartment buildings in a middle-class neighborhood.

We entered the apartment complex building directly across from the suspect's apartment. We took the elevator to the top floor. After ringing the door, Octavio's friend and his wife invited us in and escorted us to their roof, an outdoor lounging area that had a barbeque pit, round picnic table with an umbrella, and two lounge chairs.

Our hosts brought us a pitcher of iced tea and told us to feel free to enter their apartment to use the restroom or telephone. They were going on vacation for a couple of weeks.

After the owners departed, we moved the table closer to the four-foot wall surrounding the roof and tipped the umbrella toward the top of the wall to make sure that the suspects would not be able to see us. We had a direct view of the suspect's second floor apartment right across the street.

Octavio took the first shift while I relaxed on one of the lounge chairs. Just as I started to doze off, Octavio told me, "Arturo, guess what. We don't have the best location. You will not believe this until you see it."

I joined him, and we saw Agent Hall park his car right in front of the suspect's apartment. He got out of his car and removed his shirt, opened the trunk, and got a small blanket that he spread on the hood of his car. He then got a set of hand barbells. He laid on his back on the hood of the car and started pumping his barbells.

As we cracked up, Octavio reminded me, "Remember, we are witnessing a Harvard graduate."

At that very moment two of the suspects came out of the apartment entrance and sat on the front cement steps approximately ten feet from Agent Hall. As we watched, the suspects stood and walked up to Jeff. They had a conversation we could not hear, but we saw Agent Hall point down the street, and the three laughed. The suspects returned to the steps, disregarding the distraction in front of them.

Shortly afterward we saw Agent Rayner and an old man walking on the sidewalk right between the suspects and Agent Hall. The old man was carrying a bottle of wine wrapped in a brown paper sack, and he offered Agent Hall a drink. He apparently refused and told them to get the hell out of his face. The old man got pissed and started telling off Agent Hall. The suspects came to Agent Hall's rescue and told them to get the hell out of there. They continued down the walk.

We maintained surveillance until 1:00 a.m., at which time the suspects took off in a taxi. They didn't have any luggage, so we relayed this information to the agents conducting roving surveillance.

All of us except Agent Rayner reported to Group Supervisor Jordan's suite for our nightly session to report our finding and get additional assignments. We told Jordan we had seen Rayner walking the area with an old drunk guy. Agent Carter and another agent went to look for him. During the meeting we asked Agent Hall what he had told the suspects that made them laugh. He said, "I told them my girlfriend was banging some other guy and that both were renting an apartment down the street and that I wanted to catch her so I could shit-can her for good."

During those midnight sessions, more guys started to be missing. On one occasion two guys got busted for speeding. Because of those no-shows, Group Supervisor Jordan got pissed off. He bitched at all of us and used the Spanish expression, "¿Porqué Yo?" (Why me?). That saying became our battle cry printed on our memorial plaque. About the same time, Miami DEA management started referring to us as the Dirty Dozen.

After conducting enough surveillance and obtaining actionable intelligence, we got a warrant to intercept telephone conversations on one of the primary targets. Because of the close proximity of the safe house wiretap to the suspect's condominium, we maintained a very low profile conducting twenty-four hour shifts and changing shifts at four in the morning.

Inside the safe house, we connected two reel-to-reel recorders to the wiretap. The first reel would be maintained as evidence. The second one was used for transcribing the conversations. Two Spanish-speaking agents monitored the tapes.

Some of the calls were humorous or downright ridiculous. For example one guy ordered "one and a half sets of white shoes." He probably wanted a kilogram and a half of cocaine.

The target yelled at him, "You asshole, what do you want them for? An amputee or what?"

Regional Director Theisen provided us with a small pool table and dart game to keep us from going stir crazy. He also kept our refrigerator full of cold cuts and other goodies.

After obtaining the needed intelligence through our wiretap and surveillance, we switched into our undercover roles, purchasing cocaine and heroin from the suspects.

I was assigned to a female informant named Lorrie (alias). She and her husband had a unique marriage. They were both gay. They were busted for cocaine trafficking, and he took the fall for both of them, resulting in his doing prison time. She agreed to cooperate in exchange for reducing her husband's prison sentence.

In setting up our undercover story, we played the role that my brother was with Lorrie's husband's roommate in prison and we were working together selling cocaine needed for attorney fees to gain a reduction of prison time for both Lorrie's husband and my alleged brother.

Lorrie and I walked into the Rancho Luna Restaurant to make contact with suspect Gilberto Hernandez. Our coffee had just been served when Gilberto walked up to us and hugged Lorrie, asking her, "Where have you been hiding, my love? I have not seen you in a long time."

She told him she has been visiting her husband in prison and then introduced me as Arturo Chavez and that my brother was in prison with her husband. Lorrie asked him to join us, which he did, after retrieving his coffee from where he had been sitting.

As previously planned, Lorrie and I agreed that during this first contact with the suspect, we would not bring up the conversation regarding drugs. She told me, "Gilberto is a greedy son of a bitch, and if we give him time, he will bring up the drug business on his own."

I excused myself to go to the restroom. In my absence, Lorrie told Gilberto that we were trying to come up with the needed money for an attorney to appeal her husband's and my brother's case. If the dialogue aroused Gilberto's attention, she would hint that we were making money through cocaine sales.

When I returned to the table, Lorrie had accomplished our

objective, because Gilberto told me, "Look, Arturo, Lorrie, whom she and her husband I consider like my brothers, just told me that you came all the way from Texas to buy cocaine. I know it is none of my business, and please don't think that I'm trying to replace your source, but I'm willing to give you a better deal.

Jokingly I told him, "Damn women. Can't keep their mouths shut."
We laughed.

As I ate my Cuban sandwich, I told him. "If you guys are that close and your stuff's purity exceeds what I'm now buying and the price is right, I certainly would consider doing business with you. I'm sure that my brother and Lorrie's husband would agree."

He invited me to the restroom, and I kidded with him, telling him, "Hey, man, I'm straight. What do you want to do in the restroom? Only girls invite each other to the restroom."

He told me, "I'm straight too, *pendejo*. I just want to give you a sample of my *perico* (cocaine). Once you check it out, you be the judge as to its high quality.

In the restroom he handed me a small packet wrapped in aluminum foil. Seeing that no one else was in the restroom, I told Gilberto. "Look, man, whatever agreement we do, it will be between you and me. I don't want to take any chances being seen with Lorrie, since she was busted with her husband. You know what I mean. I wanted to tell you this alone, because I don't want to hurt her feelings. Okay?"

"Got you, man. I'll join you guys shortly. I have to take a dump."

I returned to the table with Lorrie and discreetly wet my finger and placed a bit of salt on my nostril. When Gilberto joined us, Lorrie told me, "Wipe that shit off your nose. What? Do you want to advertise to the whole world?"

I obediently wiped my nose and told Gilberto, "Man, you appear to be a man of your word. Your stuff is really good, but I expect that the entire amount that I purchase from you will all be the same quality as the sample. Okay, let's now talk price."

He said, "Fine, usually at about this time of the day you will find

CHAPTER 15

me here having breakfast, or if you want, have Lorrie call me. You just let me know how much you want, and I will have it. I'm selling it at $35,000.00 a kilo."

"That is good enough for me, *amigo*. Look, tomorrow I will buy a quarter kilo from you at about this same time here. Let's see, that would be at $8,750.00, right?"

"Got it right. See you here tomorrow at about this time."

I came alone the following day, with the exception of the discreet surveillance, and met Gilberto accompanied by a younger guy he introduced as Jaime. Gilberto said, "Look, man, I don't want to piss you off, but I'm heavy into Santeria. Following the vibes I got from my last night's prayer session, I got a message that I should not make a hand-to-hand transaction."

I had heard about the Cuban Santeria ritual that was a semi-religious cult practiced in the Caribbean Islands. Some of the Cuban drug traffickers claimed a certain reverence to Santeria and placed a glass half full of water on a mini altar and placed a half-smoked cigar on top of the glass. Usually they did this ritual before they made a drug sale.

I played the ignorant role that I didn't know what the hell Gilberto was talking about and told him, "What do you suggest, that we wait until Christmas and have Santa Claus deliver me the stuff?"

He laughed, then said, "No, what I mean is that today Jaime will go to the restroom and get into one of the stalls, and you will follow him and get into the second one. He will hand you the quarter kilo, and you give him the money. Once he counts the money to see it is complete, he will leave. Once you check the quarter kilo to your satisfaction, you can take off, okay?"

"No problem, *mi amigo*. Let's do it, because I have other shit to do today."

Jaime and I got into the toilet stalls and exchanged the quarter kilo of cocaine for the money and went our separate ways after checking everything was right. The agents on surveillance saw Jaime give Gilberto the money after I left the café.

A week later I telephoned Gilberto and told him that I was ready to purchase the kilogram of cocaine for $35,000. I told him, "Last time we did the thing at your location. This time we will do it at mine. There is a pier on the southern side of the Haulover Inlet. It's a place lots of people go fishing. I will have the money in a fishing tackle box, and you can bring the kilo in something like a bait bucket or something like that. I will be there this Sunday at noon.

Gilberto said, "I know the location exactly. My grandfather used to take me fishing there when I was a kid. I'll be there."

On Sunday I showed up at the pier with a fishing pole and an old fishing tackle box Agent Octavio Gonzalez found in his garage. It contained the $35,000 dollars. Octavio accompanied me.

Gilberto arrived in his new Corvette and got out carrying a bucket. He sat next to me on the pier and said, "There are too many people here. Let's do the transfer in our cars."

I said, "That's a good idea, but I want you to know that my brother-in-law is waiting for me in the car. If it's okay with you, I'll introduce you to him. If I can't come on future transactions, he is my representative, and you can deal with him."

Gilberto said, "No problem, but for now I want you to open your car's rear window, and I will drop the kilo on the backseat. You just put your tackle box with the money on the ground, and I will pick it up from there. Remember, no hand-to-hand exchanges."

"Got you, my man."

At the car I introduced Agent Gonzales to Gilberto as I lowered the rear door window. Gilberto dumped the kilogram of cocaine on the backseat and picked my tackle box from the ground and took it to his car. After he counted the money, he blinked his lights, and we both went our separate ways.

During this time frame, several other task force agents made undercover drug purchases.

Sometime after that, it was determined that our Dirty Dozen team was having too many problems being together twenty-four hours of the day. We were informed that we would be able to have our families join us at our own per-diem expense.

This idea was an excellent one, and I found a nice condo in the Miami Beach area so the kids would be able to enjoy the beach. On the first Sunday, after we went to Mass, Mariana fixed us a great breakfast. She opened the small kitchen window, and the bacon aroma made its way to the neighbors. Shortly afterward the elderly Jewish landlady, accompanied by her teenage grandson, knocked on our door and told us that we had to leave immediately because our condo had been rented to us in error. While she said this, her grandson, a step behind her, waved his hand back and forth, letting us know she was lying.

Because of my undercover role, I decided not to make it an issue, and we departed. Agent Gonzalez quickly found us a nice condo with a swimming pool on Flagger Street in Miami. I started teaching the girls and Gino how to swim. Andrew refused my instructions and just sat on the poolside with his feet dangling into the water. All he did was watch the rest of the family trying to swim. On the third day, he woke up and told us. "Let's go outside. I know how to swim."

We went to the pool and Andrew dove into it and swam across to the other side. Since then we have taken what he says more seriously.

We reported to the Miami BNDD office for the last time, also early in the morning, to be assigned to the raiding and arrest teams. I noticed that all the Dirty Dozen team members except me got their assignments. Just as I was about to bitch about it, Regional Director Theisen pointed his finger at me and said, "Sedillo, follow me to my office to get your assignment."

I followed him into his office, where he pointed to a miniature statue of an elephant on his desk and asked me, "Do you know what this represents?"

"The Republican Party?"

"Wrong. It represents the mind that does not forget, and I have not forgotten when you attended a FBN/State Police conference in Long Beach, California, and you intervened on behalf of the Mexican

Federal Police and our Commissioner Giordano regarding opening an office in Guadalajara, Mexico, right?"

"Yes, sir."

"Well, Art, after this operation, you guys will be given the choice of duty stations, and I was hoping you would consider our office. For that reason I didn't want you on the arrest teams, so you could continue working undercover. What I want you to do now is to work the streets and hang outs of the suspects. We are sure once we make the first arrests, the word will spread out and some of the suspects will attempt to get the hell out of the area. Your job is to radio in any information regarding any potential fugitive."

I thanked him for asking me to select Miami and told him that I was planning for a foreign assignment such as Mexico City, but if I didn't get it, I would be happy to select his office. He smiled and told me to get the hell out of his office.

More than 117 suspects were arrested nationwide on that day, including eighteen in the Florida area. After the raid, we got our choice of assignments. Our boss, Group Supervisor Hector Jordan, was assigned to the Madrid, Spain, BNDD Attaché, and Agent Octavio was assigned to Bogota, Colombia, Gordon Rayner got Paraguay. I got Mexico City.

My family and I had a wonderful drive back to Texas except for one incident. Throughout the trip our five-year-old, Gino, kept talking to his teddy bear named Joey. After a nap, he woke up and couldn't find Joey. We stopped at a rest area and looked for Joey with negative results. The last time Joey was seen was when Gino took him to the restroom at a gas station in Alabama. No way were we going to backtrack a hundred miles. He hated Alabama through most of his childhood.

CHAPTER 16

THE FOLLOWING MONDAY at our Dallas Regional Office weekly meeting, Regional Director Karadimos complimented me on my Miami assignment and handed me two headquarters teletypes confirming my promotion to GS-11 and my reassignment to Mexico City BNDD under the command of Regional Director Joe Arpaio.

This was a short and joyous day, and once I finished my pending administrative work, I bid my friends farewell and went home to pack and ship our furniture to Mexico City.

When the movers' eighteen-wheeler departed, we drove to New Mexico to spend a few days with relatives before continuing to Mexico City.

I telephoned my Chihuahua, Mexico, friend, Prosecutor Leon Delgado, that we were on our way to Mexico City and invited him and his wife to have dinner with us at the Chihuahua Hotel where we would be stopping overnight. He said, "Under no circumstances. We insist that you stay with us and have supper at our house."

I told him we would have supper with them, but we would have to stay at the hotel per traveling orders. He told me he knew the owner of the hotel where we were staying, and he would be standing by for us at that location.

Once we were on the road, the reality of being transferred to a foreign post kicked in. Mariana and I erred in not intensifying the kids' Spanish-speaking abilities. She attempted to cram Spanish 101 in Athena and Rita by reciting to them "Water-*aqua*, bread-*pan*," etc. She didn't include Andrew and Gino, figuring she would teach them at home in Mexico City.

When we arrived at Chihuahua, Leon was standing by for us at the hotel. After we checked in, we followed him to his residence, a hacienda-type house with a walled-in landscaped yard. When he opened the wooden gate, we were surprised by the applause of his family and friends, who included a Mariachi group playing the traditional welcoming song.

His wife had prepared a wonderful dinner, and we had a great time. Not only was Leon a prominent public official, but on that evening we learned that he was an accomplished musician and composer as well.

After the mariachis played the *despidida* (farewell) song, Leon told us, "Driving into Mexico City can be a traumatic experience, even for us nationals. It is one of the biggest cities in the world. I do not want to interfere with your plans, but I want you to know that it would be my pleasure and honor to help you drive the rest of the way to Mexico City.

"At the same time," he said, "I will familiarize you with our federal government structure, particularly with the entities you will be working with, including the attorney general's office and the Federal Judicial Police."

"Leon, you must be psychic," I said. "Mariana and I were concerned about all those things, and it would be our pleasure to have you accompany us."

The following morning Leon joined us, and our trip became most educational because of his priceless briefings. He not only explained the federal and local political party structure but also went into the historical and cultural development from the Aztec civilization to the present.

When we approached Mexico City, Leon insisted on driving so that I would be able to better appreciate the view without having to worry about the hectic traffic. As we approached the famous Paseo de la Reforma Avenue, we marveled at the beauty of the countless Mexican heroic statues bordering both sides of the street.

Leon pointed out a beautiful five-story marble building surrounded by a tall wrought iron fence. He said, "That's where you will be working."

Half a block past the U.S. Embassy, we parked near the Angel statue and went into the Sanborn Café. After changing into a dress shirt and tie and passing Mariana's and Leon's inspection, I left them there eating while I walked to the U.S. Embassy.

On that August 28, 1970, a Friday, at about 3:00 p.m., I paused momentarily in front of the beautiful massive marble building. As a slight breeze waved our American Flag, I felt goosebumps on my arms thinking that this was a long way from the West Las Vegas Police Department where I had initiated my law enforcement career. As I said a silent prayer, I also realized that if it hadn't been for the love of my life, Mariana, who had caused my being hired by the New Mexico State Police, I would not be standing where I was.

A Mexican National Security Guard approached me from within the gate and asked the nature of my visit. After I identified myself with my BNDD badge and passport, he opened the gate and escorted me to the U.S. Marine post.

After I showed the Marine guard my credentials, he called the BNDD office to have an agent escort me to the office. While waiting I told the Marine "Simper Fi," to let him know that I'm a former U.S. Marine. His stern expression converted into a big smile, and we shook hands while he welcomed me aboard.

A tall agent named Tom Waddell showed up and with a big smile welcomed me, telling me, "Agent Jack Compton and I are sure happy you have arrived so that we can get Regional Director Arpaio off our asses and on new meat."

We took the elevator to the fourth floor and on to our offices, where he introduced me to Deputy Assistant Agent Jack Compton. He was another tall cowboy-looking guy. After exchanging greetings, he escorted me to Regional Director Joe Arpaio's Office.

Regional Director Arpaio was sitting behind his massive desk with an unlit half-smoked cigar sticking out of his mouth. The other guys had warned me not to say shit about his cigar.

Common knowledge was widespread that Regional Director Arpaio was a hard-ass supervisor, so I played it cool and walked in like a humble subordinate. He cracked what appeared to be half a smile and told me, "Don't pay attention to whatever those guys said about me." As he spoke, he extended a handshake, welcoming me.

After a short briefing, he said, "You must be tired after that long drive, so I'm going to cut you loose so you can join your family and enjoy the weekend. Tell our secretary, Mrs. Joan Banister, to give you information regarding your temporary quarters, which is an apartment building half a block behind the embassy. Get your family settled in and enjoy the weekend. Come with your family on Monday morning at 9:00 a.m., so we can get you all processed.

As he dismissed me I felt that regardless what the other agents had warned me about the man, I felt that we would have a good working relationship.

Mrs. Banister gave me the apartment key and walked with me to a rear corner office space assigned to me. Through the window she pointed out the general area of the apartment located on Roma Street half a block behind the embassy.

I joined my family and Leon, and after eating, we drove around the block to our apartment and parked the vehicle in the basement, where the landlord was standing by for us. He escorted us up to the second-floor apartment. It had a nice balcony with comfortable lounge chairs.

After settling down, we took the manager's advice and walked half a block down the street to a large super Mercado to purchase groceries. On our way back we picked up freshly made corn and flour tortillas from the shop next to our apartment.

On the following morning, I drove Leon to the bus depot, where he departed for Chihuahua.

We continued enjoying our weekend, attending Mass at a small Catholic church located half a block across from the U.S. Embassy. We took the landlord's advice, and after Mass took a local taxi to Chapultepec Park, which was on a lake and has several outdoor cafés. We walked across the street and enjoyed visiting the famous Mexican National Museum of Anthropology.

Back at our apartment we enjoyed the evening breeze while we sat on our balcony viewing the local traffic. Beside the normal traffic we noticed several vendors traveling on bicycles, and each has a particular whistle to identify its product.

The kids' favorite vendor was the one that sold fresh half-peeled mangos with red chili salsa. Each time the kids heard that vendor's particular whistle, they would rush downstairs with a peso to buy a mango. Athena learned how to mimic the mango vendor whistle and would hide and whistle. The other kids would rush downstairs to find no vendor.

On Monday morning we went to the U.S. Embassy, and Mrs. Banister took care of processing the family and cut me loose to join Agent Waddell, who told me, "It's too early to start working. Let me show you our usual morning drill."

We took the elevator to the basement floor where we picked up a cup of coffee and joined Agent Compton on the cafeteria patio, where he was having a full breakfast.

They both continued briefing me and joking, telling me to make every effort to stay out of Arpaio's field of vision and that I would have to do it for only a week or so, at which time two or three more agents would be arriving.

Back in the office I learned Mrs. Banister had processed my family with all the necessary documents, and my family had been released to return to the apartment.

Regional Director Arpaio was standing by his office door and with a shitty smile told me, "Like I told you, don't believe all the shit these guys said about me."

I responded with a "Yes, sir."

Before hitting the streets, I went through the usual office orientation and administrative stuff. Regional Director Arpaio then gave me a more through briefing. "Remember that you are in a foreign country, and you will not have the luxury of having multi-law enforcement agencies at your call like back in the States. This is a dangerous environment, and you are expected to take all the needed precautions. Most of the time you will be working by yourself with our counterparts, the Mexican Federal Judicial Police (MFJP)."

Before hitting the streets, I went through the usual U.S. Embassy seminar attended by all mission newcomers in which the ambassador and other officials welcomed us aboard and reminded us of expected protocol.

A couple of weeks later agents Humberto "Burt" Moreno and Amadeo "Art" Medina and their families arrived. Medina was a fellow New Mexican from Mora, a small village near my Las Vegas hometown. He and I became good friends and worked as partners whenever possible.

Agent Moreno had a bit more time on the job than us and turned out to be a bit political in the sense that he bullshitted us all that he was related to one of the Mexican deputy attorney generals. Regional Director Arpaio made him his official translator, since the boss's Spanish was limited.

On September 13, 1970, Regional Director Arpaio gave me my first assignment, to accompany the Mexican Deputy Attorney General Franco Rodriguez to Acapulco, Mexico, to witness a ceremonial burning of several tons of marijuana and opium plants.

Arpaio instructed me, "Go to the airport and ask for directions to

First Commander Arturo Durazo's office, and when you get to him, tell him that you are the U.S. Embassy representative to accompany the deputy attorney general to the Acapulco drug-burning ceremony."

As I rode in a taxi to the airport, I thought, "Shit, here all of a sudden I will be rubbing shoulders with the number-two guy in the Mexican attorney general's office instead of working the streets with my regular counterpart agents."

I was a bit nervous, but when I got to Commander Durazo's office and introduced myself, he was most gracious and right away fixed me a tequila shot to join them in pre-celebration of the next day's Mexican Independence Day celebration.

Shortly afterward Deputy Attorney General Franco, a distinguished-looking man in his late sixties arrived. After we exchanged greetings and I told him that I was assigned to accompany him, he too was most gracious and told me as we exchanged macho hugs, "Don Arturo, in our law enforcement business we don't have the luxury of establishing a gradual and time-consuming relationship. We recognize each other at face value and hope for the best that we can create a meaningful, professional, and friendly relationship."

Damn, such elegance. I was almost speechless and finally responded, "Sir, I concur totally with what you said. It is indeed my pleasure meeting you, and I assure you that I intend to establish that meaningful relationship you have mentioned."

We gave a toast to both our countries and our relationship with another tequila drink. He then asked me to sit next to him in the aircraft so we could get to know each other better.

Upon arriving at the Acapulco airport, our delegation received a high-profile armed guard escort to the VIP room where the deputy attorney general made a small speech to the news media. We then continued with police motorcycle escort to a rustic palm-tree café in Acapulco right on the beach.

We were served an excellent seafood meal and beverages. As we ate, several Mexican Army soldiers unloaded an eighteen-wheeler flatbed truck with several tons of marijuana and opium plants, piling them for the bonfire ceremony.

When I finished eating, I don't know if I diplomatically screwed up, but I removed my Guayabera shirt and joined the soldiers unloading the truck.

Upon seeing me, Don Franco ordered the MFJP agents and their supervisors to join me in assisting the soldiers. They didn't seem thrilled getting the order but complied.

When we finished we returned to our tables while the soldiers got under the truck to rest and protect themselves from the blazing sun.

I walked to Don Franco and said, "Sir, with all due respect, there remains a lot of food on the table. Is it possible that the waiters serve it to the tired soldiers?"

Don Franco patted me on my shoulder and ordered the servers to take the food to the soldiers. Several soldiers gave me a thumb's up in appreciation. Little did I know then that sometime after, some of those soldiers would come to my rescue.

After the burning ceremony, we returned to the Mexico City airport. Don Franco saw me walking toward the taxi stand and insisted on having his agent drop me off at my residence. After MFJP Agent Francisco Benavidez Zarate dropped Don Franco at his residence, he drove me to the Roma Street apartment. Francisco and his wife Teresa became our good friends.

CHAPTER 17

CELEBRATING THE MEXICAN Independence Holiday is almost as sacred as religion, and the majority of people suffer hangovers after it. When we returned to work on September 18, 1979, most of us were still nursing our hangovers and maintained a low profile. Group Supervisor Jack Compton instructed me, "Art, we got a call from the Marine Post that a well-dressed gentleman is requesting to talk to us. Check him out, and if he looks legit, bring him up."

I checked out the visitor, processed the guy through the Marine Post, and brought him up to my office after establishing that he was a community leader and had information regarding a drug trafficking organization. We will call the source Juan. Juan told me, "Shit, man, I discreetly came here to talk to you guys, and I have been standing here for the past half hour with all these damn people eyeballing me."

He was referring to the nationals standing in the visa application line. I apologized. "The moment I was told you were here I rushed down for you. Sorry for the delay. How can I help you?"

"It's more of a matter of me helping you guys regarding some idiots that are pushing dope and using young kids to smuggle the shit into your country."

He requested assurance that his identify would be kept confidential, which I assured him it would, as long as he was straight with us.

He said, "I know two guys, a Mexican named Enrique Montano and a black Venezuelan named Pedro. I don't know his last name. Those two have a heroin and marijuana provider in Acapulco. Anyway, I bullshitted them that I had met a guy at a commercial conference I attended at El Paso, Texas, who was interested in buying large amounts of heroin and marijuana. I may have jumped the gun in attempting to set up the pushers to meet you guys in your undercover roles."

I kidded him, "Are you sure you didn't miss your calling and should have become a narcotics enforcement agent with your government?"

He said, "Better yet, recruit me into your country, and I'll become an agent. Now really, the fact is that I told the pushers that the guy I had met was here in town and would be willing to meet them this afternoon at 6:00."

Realizing that Juan appeared to be a reliable person, I documented him as my first foreign Cooperating Individual (CI) and relayed his information to Group Supervisor Compton, telling him that I was willing to meet the two suspects at the Sanborn Café. He agreed and sent two guys to conduct surveillance on the meeting. The guys were grateful for having a legitimate excuse to go get a couple of Tecate beers to cure their hangovers while they kept an eye on the suspects and me.

We telephoned Enrique to confirm the meeting at 6:00 at the Sanborn Café near the Angel Statue on Paseo De La Reforma Street. We escorted Juan out of the embassy through the rear exit so that no one would see him leaving.

At the next-door Maria Isabella Hotel I made a reservation using my alias with our hotel contact in the event the suspects telephoned to confirm that I was a registered guest. At 6:00 I walked into Sanborn Café and found the informant sitting with Pedro and Enrique. The first thing that came to my mind was how odd the two looked as a team. Pedro was a light-colored black guy with hazel eyes. He looked more like an athlete than a dope pusher. Enrique, on the other hand, was a pudgy Mexican with shabby neck-length black hair and a poorly maintained goatee.

After introductions we all ordered steak sandwiches and Tecate beers.

Enrique was a load mouth and attempted to give himself self-importance until Pedro smiled at him and told him to shut up.

We had a general conversation of how the C.I. and I knew each other and how I was interested in finding a better connection to purchase multi kilograms of heroin and tons of marijuana if the price and quality were right. I also stated that I was more interested in having a reliable source that could provide me the large amounts I would be purchasing on a regular basis.

Pedro asked me what I was a currently paying for a ton of marijuana and a kilogram of heroin.

I told him, "Look, man, I have laid out my conditions, so please, and with all due respect, I can understand a bit of bartering, but like I told you guys, I don't need a new source unless it is safe and financially beneficial to me. I need to know the cost and quality."

Pedro smiled and said, "Okay, you damn *gringos* are hard to negotiate with. Okay, if you buy the marijuana by the ton, calculate each kilogram for ninety pesos—that's seven US dollars, so for the five tons it would come out as thirty-five thousand American dollars."

I kidded him, "What, you have a computer up your ass that figured both the weight and currency exchanges?"

"No man, it's that we deal with these figures all the time selling to you Americans. Now regarding the kilogram of heroin. Since the opium is not harvested yet, we can't set a price until we find out the status of the crop."

"That's fine with me."

Enrique said, "Look, Arturo, our marijuana and opium cultivations are in the Guererro Mountains about a hundred kilometers north of Acapulco. We will have to talk with our people to see if they will let you check out the cultivations and supplies. Once we get their approval, we can get back to you to confirm or tell you we can't do it, okay? Once we find out, we will get back to you through Juan."

I told him, "Is there any way I can be in direct contact with you guys? I thank Juan for getting us together, but I believe in minimizing the people involved once we get going with our transactions."

Enrique gave me his telephone number and requested that I call him in the afternoons, because he was a late sleeper. We exchanged farewells and went our separate ways.

On the following week I met Enrique and Pedro alone at Danny's Café, a block from the U.S. Embassy. I flashed them with a briefcase full of twenty-dollar bills, telling them that I was showing them several thousands of dollars to let them know that I was not bullshitting them. After showing them the money, I excused myself for a while and took the suitcase to Agents Moreno and Medina, who were standing by in the restroom.

Enrique told me that he had obtained his people's approval for me to travel with him to the Acapulco area, where we would meet with the nephew of their major source of supply. The nephew was named Torres. Once we met Torres, he would call his uncle, Don Salvador, who would give the final approval for me to see their illicit plantations and stockpiles.

I told Pedro and Enrique that once I saw the cultivations and stockpile I would pay them a five-hundred-dollar finder's fee.

On the following morning Enrique was punctual, carrying an overnight bag and standing by for me at the Maria Isabella Hotel lobby. We took a taxi to the airport and a flight to Acapulco, Mexico.

Group Supervisor Jack Compton and TDY DEA Agent Gordon Rayner accompanied MFJP agents Commander Ernesto Guereña, Agent Sanchez Nieda, and Agent Arturo Garces, and the commander's assistant, Joselito. They traveled to Acapulco, Mexico, and registered into the Presidente Hotel. They and the military would be coordinating the investigation.

When Enrique and I arrived at the Acapulco airport, he rented a car and dropped me off at the Presidente Hotel and continued to a local motel. It was agreed that in an hour he would pick me up so that we could meet with Torres before we continued to the Petatlan area to meet Don Salvador to observe the drugs and cultivations.

When I got off the elevator on the third floor after telephoning Agent Compton from the lobby that I was on my way up, MFJP Agent Sanchez Nieda scared the shit out of me by sneaking behind me and grabbing me, holding me tight. He burst out laughing, and we exchanged macho hugs. He was my buddy whom I had met at the Long Beach, California, FBN/State Police conference several years before. Actually that meeting with him and FBN National Commissioner Harry Giordano resulted in my being hired by FBN.

I briefed the team on the status of my ongoing undercover operation. I informed them that suspect Enrique would come for me, shortly, to take me to Petatlan so that I could see the illicit cultivations and stockpiles.

When Enrique picked me up we drove to a motel cafeteria where we sat with Torres, who would interview me and evaluate whether he would authorize Enrique to take me to his uncle, Don Salvador.

Torres, a guy in his early twenties wearing a gold necklace and a Rolex watch, played the bad ass role, warning me that I'd better not be associated with the police. Not letting him intimidate me, I responded, "Your intentions better not be to rip off my money, because my people will take care of you. Now are we going to bullshit each other, or are we going to talk business?"

That comment did the trick, and he calmed down, telling Enrique to go ahead and take me to his uncle, Don Salvador.

Enrique and I continued on our trip but somewhat delayed our arrival because of a tropical storm. We arrived at Petatlan at 6:00 p.m. to a still sunny evening.

Petatlan was such a small village that I was surprised that it merited a name. Most of the area had fruit trees and other legitimate cultivations, including pineapples and coconuts. The village was right on the Pacific Coast. The highway ran between the coast and the plantations to the foot of a mountain.

Enrique drove up a dirt road to Don Salvador's residence, a house concealed behind brush and a five-foot rock wall that had an iron gate.

He honked the horn, and shortly afterward, Don Salvador and two guys armed with AK-47 rifles approached us. A third guy was carrying a sack full of marijuana.

Don Salvador, a man in his forties, but who appeared older because of a scar running diagonally across his sunburned face, acknowledged me with a head shake. He told Enrique, "Have Jorge bring him up to me tomorrow morning." Enrique said okay and paid him for the sack of marijuana. They all returned to the house without another word said.

While Enrique drove me to Jorge's home, he told me that he would have to drop me off at Jorge's and he would be taking the sack of marijuana to a client standing by for him at Cuernavaca, Mexico. He told me once Jorge took me to see Don Salvador's drug stashes and cultivations, I was to take a bus back to Acapulco where he and Pedro would be standing by for their finder's fee and to coordinate the delivery of the five tons of marijuana.

Dropping me off in the middle of nowhere was not to my liking, but then again I couldn't do anything, because the suspects were complying with what we had agreed to.

We drove right to the beach area where Jorge lived in a rustic palm branch beach shack with his wife and two young daughters. The peasant Jorge Brito, who was about twenty-five years old, wore cut-off faded Levi shorts and was shirtless and barefooted. He was mending a fishing net that was stretched out between two palm trees.

After introductions and telling Jorge that I'm the guy he would be taking to the Don Salvador camp the following morning, Enrique told me, "Once you see what you came to see, Jorge will walk you to the village bus stop for you to return to Acapulco, where we will be waiting for you.

After Enrique departed, both Jorge and I just stayed there speechless for a while until he said, "I think that we can both agree on one thing, and that is that Enrique is a *pendejo* (stupid guy)."

We both laughed, agreeing.

He walked me to his hut and introduced me to his wife and two young daughters. Jorge turned out to me a pleasant and hospitable person. He told me to take off my tennis shoes so we could go catch supper. He handed me one of his two homemade bamboo fishing poles and we walked on the beach a short distance to a freshwater cove that poured into the ocean.

He walked to a small waterfall and took two cold Tecate beers from a bucket. In a short time we caught three nice sized snappers as we enjoyed our beers. His wife got the homemade barbeque pit going and fried the fish with vegetables. We had a great supper with the fish and had pineapple slices for dessert. Under other circumstances I would have considered this event pleasurable.

That night after the candles were blown out, Jorge hung two hammocks from palm trees about four feet apart and told me, "Don Arturo, I know we just met, and I hope that what I tell you will not offend you."

"I have bad breath or what?"

He laughed and said, "No, what I want to tell you is that all my life I have been a hard-working God-fearing man and have done everything within my limited abilities to provide for my family. A while ago I noticed you dropped your rosary, and you quickly picked it up and hid it in your pocket. That in itself told me you are a good man."

"Thank you. I also think that you are an honorable person and apparently a good family man."

He continued, "I'm telling you all this so you can know how I got involved with Enrique and the rest of these people. About a couple of months ago my youngest daughter became very sick. We figured that spoiled milk might have poisoned her or something. The local medical doctor is a worthless drunk who mostly specializes in stitching stabbings and bullet wounds. My daughter continued with diarrhea and vomiting, so I took her on the bus to a clinic in Acapulco.

"At the clinic I was arguing with the receptionist who wanted to charge me more than the small amount of money I had. I told her we were from Petatlan, and I promised to pay her the balance later on.

"While I was arguing with her, Pedro and Enrique came into the clinic with a guy who had been stabbed. They overheard my conversation with the receptionist.

"Enrique walked up to me and asked, 'Pardon me, did you say you were from Petatlan?'

"I said, 'That's right. I'm a humble worker and my daughter is very sick, but they will not take care of her.

"Enrique takes out a fat roll of pesos and peels off a thousand pesos and hands them to the receptionist and instructs her, 'Take care of this man's daughter, and if more is needed, let me know.'

"Besides that, Enrique hands me another thousand pesos so that I can eat and have a place to stay while my daughter was hospitalized. I promised to pay him back.

"While we were waiting for the results of both our patients, Enrique asked me if I knew Don Salvador. I told him that I do and that as a matter of fact he is one of my clients. I told him that I sell him fertilizer for his Petatlan house garden. I explained to them that I collect manure and mix it with other chemicals and sell the fertilizer to several local Petatlan farmers. This is hard work, since I don't have a car and have to walk to several ranches where they let me collect the fertilizer, and then I have to deliver it to the different clients, including Don Salvador.

"After talking for a while longer, Enrique asked me, 'How would you like to make a lot more money and less work?'

"I told them that it would be like a miracle and my prayers being answered.

"Enrique told me, 'All you would have to do is go up the mountain empty-handed to Don Salvador's camp and bring down a sack of marijuana and take the bus over here to Acapulco. This would be easier work than what you are doing now, and we will pay you much more than what you are making now, working your ass off.'

"Well, to make a long story short, for the past two months I have been hauling marihuana sacks down from Don Salvador's mountain stash and taking them on the midnight bus to Acapulco, where Pedro and Enrique pay me. The only problem that I have is being caught by the *federales* or the military, which could mean death, leaving my family abandoned."

As I listened to Jorge, I sympathized with his situation but was careful not to expose my undercover role. I told him. "You know, Jorge, I have a feeling that you are a good person and maybe I will be able to help you."

He thanked me and added, "I want you to know that I didn't know whether to tell you what I just said, but I too felt that you are a good man. I hope that we keep this conversation secret."

"Jorge, don't worry one bit. I will not tell those *pendejos* anything. After this negotiation, I'm thinking of dropping them as middlemen in my business."

He said, "I give you my word of honor that what we said will be our secret. Now, Arturo, we have to go to sleep, because tomorrow we will be climbing that gigantic mountain across the street."

We both said, "*Buenas noches*" and fell asleep.

At five in the morning, Jorge gently tapped me on my shoulder and said, "Get up, Arturo. Let's go freshen up in the ocean, but this early you can't go too deep unless you want to become a shark's breakfast."

After a refreshing bath, we had a good breakfast, and then Jorge somewhat changed my wardrobe to blend in with the local *compesino* community. He lent me a used white shirt and tire-sole handcrafted sandals plus a worn-out straw hat.

Armed with machetes, we walked across the highway and beyond the coconut plantations to the foot of the mountain and a narrow trail through the jungle-like environment.

As we started the forty-five-degree climb, I began to bitch.

Jorge told me, "Arturo, preserve your strength by not talking. Every once in a while we will take a break."

On one of those breaks we continued the previous night's conversation. Jorge told me, "Arturo, with your English speaking and my knowledge of fishing, we could buy a boat and get out of this business. We could have fishing expeditions for tourists or we could sell the fish to the Acapulco market."

I responded, "You know, guy that sounds like an excellent idea and strangely enough, I was more or less thinking of getting out of this business. After this deal, let's further discuss this."

He broke into a big smile and said, "Okay, now let's stop talking, because soon Don Salvador and his henchmen will be meeting us."

One good thing going for us was a little natural creek that paralleled the trail from which we drank periodically. After a while I came up with a bright idea and started walking in the creek to cool off somewhat. Jorge kept telling me not to do it, but I ignored him.

About an hour afterward, I realized why I should have paid attention to his warnings. The nails penetrated through the sandal's soles and punctured the bottom of my feet. We had to take an extensive break while Jorge flattened out the penetrating nails with a rock. He then searched and found medicinal leaves that I applied to my feet.

We continued climbing for an additional half hour, when we hear someone chopping the brush up front. Jorge yelled, "Don Salvador, it's me, Jorge."

Don Salvador and two of his armed guards popped out of the brush, and one told us, "Damn, we were about to give up waiting for you."

Jorge, pointing to my feet, said, "This stupid gringo kept walking in the creek and didn't pay attention to me, and the nails tore the shit out of his feet. We had to stop and fix both him and the sandals."

"I'm not a gringo. I'm what they call back in the States a Chicano, which is a Mexican American."

Don Salvador smiled as he told one of his men to go for one of the horses and told us to take a break and rest a while. His man returned with a horse, and they helped me get on it, and we continued up the mountain to the crest to a camouflaged tent about ten feet by forty feet long. The sides were rolled up. Two large camping tables stretched out inside, where four other guys played cards or just took it easy. Bed rolls and hammocks hung from the sides.

Don Salvador didn't bother introducing me to the men, and we acknowledged each other with a simple hand wave. Jorge had told me that those men were Don Salvador's cultivators and guards.

Don Salvador had me climb into one of the hammocks, and he pulled a wooden rocking chair near me and sat. He handed me a cold Tecate beer and had one of his men bring a first aid kid and instructed him to take care of my feet. When the guy finished, I thanked him, and he left.

Don Salvador told me, "I'm going to be very frank with you. I hate that damn Enrique and his Negro partner. Each time we deal with them, they cheat us by paying us a low price and then they jack up the price to their clients. This is the first time I met one of their clients; that is to say, you. I would prefer to deal with you directly."

There was no way I was going to disagree with my dangerous host. I told him, "Don Salvador, you will not believe it, but I want you to know that I didn't like them myself. You can verify what Jorge and I talked about these guys and came to the same conclusion. I would very much like to deal with you directly, and we can do that; however, I did promise those guys a finder's fee, which I will honor and pay them five hundred dollars. I'm doing it to make sure they don't get pissed and double-cross us."

Don Salvador agreed to deliver me the five tons of marijuana when I arrived with a truck in a couple of days. He told me Jorge would guide me to his house when we were ready to make the transaction.

Don Salvador broke into a big smile, and we shook hands. Jorge joined us and confirmed that we had the same conversation regarding Pedro and Enrique.

Don Salvador had me mount the horse. He and Jorge walked by my side to a shack that had a rear wall that was the side of the mountain. We walked into the shack that served as a guard post. It had a hammock next to an open window. Through the window his men guarded the opium and marihuana plants.

The rear of the shed opened to a gigantic cave where several tons of marihuana were stored in kilogram packages. There was a metal packing machine, thick rolls of metal bailing strips, and a gas-powered generator.

I told Don Salvador, "Sir, this is most impressive, and I can assure you that I will never doubt your word and I'm looking for a long and profitable relationship."

He pointed out the several hectares of opium plants, assuring me a yearly harvest conversion to 200 kilograms of heroin.

We returned to the camp for supper. After that he had me rest a while more. Late that evening we shook hands, and he had his men guide us back on another trail that ended south of Petatlan. Before I departed, Don Salvador told me that if there was a short delay in responding to us when we come for the five tons, it would be because of a commitment he had in the near village of Atoyac.

I was glad the horse was made available to me again. A guide handed me a flashlight, and we made our way to the downhill trail. I kept bitching because branches kept hitting me on the face. The guide came back to me and told me, "You dumb shit, I gave you the flashlight so that you can see ahead of yourself and wave the branches out of the way. You don't point the flashlight down front for the horse's sake. He knows the trail by heart."

The three had a good laugh, but I did take his advice, and the rest of the trip was more pleasant.

When we reached the roadside, the guide jumped on the horse and galloped up the trail. We waited for about a couple of hours for the midnight bus that Jorge waved down. The beat-up bus was almost full, mostly with peasants carrying vegetables to market or returning to their maid and handyman jobs. I finally felt relaxed, thanked God and Saint Jude for keeping me safe, and we swiftly fell asleep like the rest of the passengers.

A couple of hours later we arrived in Acapulco and took a taxi to the Presidente Hotel. The tourists were just returning from night-clubbing or whatever. They looked at us kind of strangely, wondering perhaps what those two dirty peasants were doing in a five-star hotel.

I lied to Jorge that I had to telephone my girlfriend and her sister to be standing by for us. Instead I telephoned Group Supervisor Jack Compton's room and told him we were on our way up and that the guide had a sack full of marijuana with him.

CHAPTER 18

As we got off the elevator, my people and the MFJP agents quickly detained both of us and separated us into different rooms. They faked beating me up while they did beat Jorge.

Once inside the room with Group Supervisor Compton, Agent Gordon Rayner, and MFJP Commander Guereña, I explained all that had taken place and apologized for the delay in returning, but that the time frame was totally out of my control. Compton told me, "You scared the shit out of us. We were giving you one more half hour before getting the military to go up the mountain looking for you."

While enjoying a hot bath, I heard a loud cry coming from the other room. I quickly put on a bathrobe and went to the connecting room and found Jorge naked and handcuffed to the shower while hot water poured on him and the MFJP agents beat the shit out of him.

I yelled at the feds, "Leave him alone! If it hadn't been for him, my life may have been endangered. He is a good man."

The whipping stopped, and while he wrapped himself in a similar robe, he looked at me in shock, probably wondering who in the hell I was, telling the authorities what to do.

After the feds apologized to Jorge, he joined me in my room, where breakfast was also ordered for him. As we ate I explained to him that I was an American narcotics enforcement agent.

Still in a bit of shock, he burst out crying and at the same time laughed telling me. "This is like a damn movie. I can't believe it."

After taking a well-deserved rest, Jorge and I joined the BNDD/MFJP Team and finished briefing them on my undercover operation. We then discussed the follow-up investigation to immobilize the Salvador organization. We learned that a Mexican Army squad was joining us for the seizure and arrest phase of the investigation.

I explained that the best approach would be to use the Trojan Horse approach, in the sense that we should rent a large canvas-covered truck and hide the Mexican Army team in it. We would also rent one of those tourist-striped taxis for our undercover team, which would include Jorge and me. We would approach Don Salvador and tell him our truck was standing by for the five tons of marijuana, and when they arrive with the marijuana, the military would jump out of the truck and arrest the suspects and follow up with locating and seizing their other illicit drug assets.

The BNDD/MFJP agreed to the plan; however, once we got together with the Army squad, their gung-ho lieutenant insisted on modifying my plan. He said that first we would go in the truck and jeep to Atoyac and look for Don Salvador at the local and only hotel in that small village. Once they located him, they would detain and interrogate him about the location of his cultivations, which would be located and destroyed.

It was obvious that the lieutenant was changing the agreed plan simply because he wanted the credit for interrogating and arresting the major suspect as well as uncovering the location of the illicit drug storage and cultivations.

According to national mandate, the MFJP is responsible for the initiation of drug enforcement activities within the cities and international borders within the republic. The military is in charge of the location and eradication of illicit cultivations growing in the mountainous terrain. As a result of this national mandate, a conflict existed between the MFJP and the Mexican Army.

The only role he gave us was that if Don Salvador was not located in Atoyac, we would revert to our Trojan Horse plan.

When we arrived at Atoyac, I got real pissed when the lieutenant ordered Jorge to accompany his team to the hotel to help them identify Don Salvador or members of his gang. While they searched, we Americans played the role of tourists and drove in the rented jeep to a local café.

An hour later the MFJP/Military team joined us, telling us that they had not found Don Salvador, but that they had detained a man possibly associated with the gang. They beat the shit out of him, but he didn't say shit. The lieutenant then said, "Okay, let's implement your plan now and go to Petatlan."

Besides me, the undercover team consisted of the jeep driver, MFJP Agent Arturo Garces; Commander Guereña, who sat in the backseat directly behind the driver; MFJP Sanchez Nieda, sitting on the back middle seat; and Group Supervisor Compton, who sat behind me. I was sitting on the right front seat. With no more room, Jorge stood on the right side bumper next to me. BNDD Agent Gordon Rayner drove our government vehicle accompanied by Jaime. The military hid in the back of the truck with the lieutenant driving it.

We drove to Petatlan, and the truck and the car parked on the side of the highway. In the jeep we continued up the hill to Don Salvador's house. It was already dusk, and in front of the house, Jorge yelled Don Salvador's name. Shortly after Don Salvador and four of his henchmen, all dressed in white pajama-type *compesino* outfits, approached us.

Jorge told him, "Don Arturo is ready to do business. The truck is parked off the highway."

Don Salvador told us. "Back up to the streetlight and wait for us there."

We backed up to the streetlight bordered by a wooden fence

between the highway and Don Salvador's house. After a few minutes, Commander Guereña alerted us, "Men, something strange is taking place here. Several people are hiding behind the fence."

The suspects started shooting at us.

A bullet hit the driver, Garces, in his left eye and in his arm. He cried in pain. Commander Guereña was shot several times, but he kept yelling for the rest of us to jump out of the jeep, and he kept returning fire, holding his rifle with one hand. I had never in my life witnessed such a selfless, brave man who was more concerned about his team than about himself.

Jack Compton and Sanchez Nieda jumped out of the backseat, and Jorge pulled me out of my seat and pushed me to the ground. We saw a shoulder-deep gully running parallel to the side of the road. We considered it a godsend and jumped into it. At the same time we saw MFJP Agent Sanchez Nieda run down the gully out of harm's way instead of joining our defense. He was the only one with an automatic shoulder weapon.

Jack Compton has a carbine rifle and I have my 38-caliber semi-automatic pistol with an extra clip. Jack and I returned fire at the suspects. Jorge also acted in a very brave manner, sticking right next to me and pointing out the location of the suspects' fire flashes coming at us.

I told Jack, "Shoot the damn light! We are sitting ducks under it."

Jack shot it, and we were better protected.

We heard one of the suspects yell at us, "You killed our commander, you sons of bitches." The corrupt local police were part of Don Salvador's gang.

Commander Guereña yelled back at them, "We are the federales, dumb fucks."

Finally after a few minutes that seemed like an hour, we heard a lot of whistles coming from down the hill. Jorge yelled at us, "Thank God, it is all over. That's the military, and when they blow their whistles, that is a message to the enemy to stop shooting or face death."

The surviving suspects dropped their weapons and came out from

DON'T EXPECT ANYTHING

behind the fence with their hands up in surrender. The military arrived and detained the survived suspects.

After this horrible experience, Jack Compton and I witnessed a most disgusting thing. MFJP Agent Sanchez, who had cowardly hidden himself during the shooting, once it was all over, came out of the trench like a bad ass. He saw one of the wounded suspects barely breathing, lying by the fence. Sanchez told him, "Let me help you." He placed his hand on the fence pole to balance himself and stood on the man's chest until he stopped breathing and died. At that very moment I lost total respect to the guy that I once considered a friend.

MFJP Agent Sanchez then argued with the Army lieutenant regarding who would evacuate the wounded agents.

At that point another hero surfaced, and that was our BNDD Agent Gordon Rayner. Totally disregarding the arguing locals, we helped him place wounded Guereña and Garces in our government vehicle, and Gordon took off to drive a hundred or more kilometers to Acapulco, Mexico, with two critically wounded agents.

The rest of us were delayed while the local magistrate conduced a judicial death hearing. He turned on the naked light bulb on his humble porch and used his kitchen table as a desk during the hearing, confirming three dead and four seriously wounded.

Needless to say, Jorge would have to say good-bye to his Petatlan beach hut and family, because the locals realized that he was part of our operation. Remaining in Petatlan was like signing his death certificate.

While the hearing was going on, Jack Compton, Jorge Brito, and I hid in the truck, accompanied by some of the soldiers. While we waited, two soldiers came up to me and told me, "We knew it was you up there in the shootout, and we told our men that we had to save your ass. You are the American diplomat who helped us unload the marijuana truck for the burning ceremony in Acapulco a couple of months ago. You also made them fed us, right?"

We hugged, and I confirmed that I was the same guy.

When we got back to Acapulco, our number-one priority was to find our wounded friends and Agent Gordon Rayner. Acapulco had no big-time medical facility or general hospitals. Instead it had several medical mini-clinics. We finally found our men at the San Felipe de Jesus Clinic.

The first person that we found was our hero, Gordon Rayner. He was entirely out, sleeping on a hall bench. He actually looked like one of the victims, in the sense that his clothing was saturated with dry blood down to his shoes. We woke him up and hugged the hell out of him.

Group Supervisor Jack Compton and I then walked into the emergency room and found our dear friends wrapped up so much that they looked like mummies. When we approached Commander Guereña, he opened his unwrapped eye and told us in English, "Brothers."

That's the first time we had heard him say anything in English. We silently cried as we acknowledged our now fraternal relationship.

It just so happened that when Agent Rayner arrived in Acapulco, he asked a taxi driver for directions, and the driver escorted him to the clinic, and a husband/wife medical team happened to be visiting the clinic. These two performed the operations on both agents. The doctor told us that good thing Commander Guerena had been shot. We were going to curse the shit out of him, when he explained, "We found a mass of cancer in his stomach and removed it. One might say if he hadn't been shot, he may have died of cancer." The doctor told us the commander had been shot seven times and Garces twice.

As we were leaving the clinic, we ran into First Commander Durazo, who yelled at us, mostly directing his comments to MFJP Agent Sanchez. He said, "Why didn't you idiots report to us what happened? We had to learn about this mess from the television."

At least Agent Sanchez then showed something like having balls and responded, "I reported what happened to our national director, so if you didn't get the word, that is not our fault."

Durazo yelled back, "You all are under house arrest, and the only

DON'T EXPECT ANYTHING

reason I'm not incarcerating you in the local jail is that these fucking Americans will bitch. I have rented a room at the La Siesta Motel for all of you to share as your house arrest. Get the hell out of my sight and stay at the motel until I release you."

Sanchez responded, "Okay, but we have to take care of one more thing before we report to the motel."

We departed to the Hotel Presidente, and I telephoned Enrique and told him I was very satisfied with what I had seen and was ready to do business for the five tons. I told him and Pedro to come to my hotel and I would be relaxing at the beach, which I well deserved. I had their five-hundred-dollar finder's fee and was ready to take delivery of the five tons. I told him to come and join me for a pineapple cocktail.

Enrique said, "We are on our way."

I put on my swimsuit, grabbed a king-size towel at poolside, and walked down to the beach and rested on a lounge chair. I told the MFJP/Military/BNDD team that when I removed the towel from my face, it would be the signal that the suspects were about to approach me.

When I saw the suspects arriving, I removed the towel from my face and the team arrested the suspects and took them to the military base. I quickly dressed and joined Group Supervisor Jack Compton and Jorge and also went to the military base. As we entered the commander's quarters, a sergeant told Jorge to sit on a hall bench and wait for us.

At the commander's office the commander saluted us and said, "We salute you for saving the lives of our federal police. My lieutenant told me your heroic battle response."

I returned the compliment, telling him, "Sir, the only reason we are alive is because of the quick response of your troops."

The commander then requested details regarding the exact location of the illicit drug cultivations and stockpiles. I looked to the hallway for Jorge to give the commander more exact information and saw that he was no longer sitting on the bench. I asked about his whereabouts, and the sergeant said, "Sir, if I'm not mistaken, they must have taken him with the other two suspects."

The commander yelled at the sergeant, "Go the hell for him. I hope it is not too late."

A moment later we heard what sounded like a firing squad.

Jack Compton and I just looked at each other in shock but were glad to see the sergeant return with Jorge, who was handcuffed and had a black cloth around his neck that had been used to blindfold his eyes.

The commanding officer pointed his finger at me and told Jorge, "You owe this man your life."

He responded, "Sir, I promise that I will help Don Arturo for the rest of my life." He did.

After this incident, we joined the rest of our team, and Jack Compton told us that we would make one more stop before reporting to our motel house arrest. He told Jaime to stop at a liquor store. We got down and loaded up with tequila, beer, and other goodies.

At the motel we threw the two mattresses on the floor to better accommodate us all. We then took turns taking a shower and telephoning our loved ones. I called Mariana, and she told me they had heard about the shootout on television, and Mrs. Banister from the office told her that she had been prohibited to comment anything to anyone until Regional Director Arpaio checked us out. She told me she and the kids had been praying for my welfare.

I told her I was okay and would be home the following day. Mariana read me a poem they had composed as they waited and prayed for my safe return:

My dad has been called
Pig, Fuzz, and Cop,
Though I've never been around
When he talks "shop."
MMM—I know he has
Led a dual life,

And because of this,
I am glad that Mommie is his wife.
Pig - Because he works in the world's sties,
Fuzz—His mean-looking beard,
But that love is still
There in his eyes.
Cop—the man we have to share
So that dope in our land will someday be rare.
I am sorry, my son, I must
Again go away.
I hear this, and I cry,
But then I'll pray.
'Cause I know he is a "narc"
And his return is unsure.
Please, Lord, bring him home soon.
His absence is hard to endure.
I am giving fair warning,
So take heed, all you pushers.
If you make him as "The Man"
Among you users,
Make sure he gets home safe and unmarked,
Because now I am small, but soon I'll grow up
And remember I am the son of that "Narc."

The follow-up investigation with MFJP and the Mexican Army resulted in the seizure and destruction of a total of fourteen tons of marijuana and seven kilograms of heroin, plus twelve hectares of illegal cultivation. According to the military, the seizure was a record.

After MFJP Commander Guereña retired he moved with his Hispanic American wife to the United States and became a U.S. citizen. His two sons became U.S. Border Patrol agents.

CHAPTER 19

OUR OFFICE INCREASED to seven agents, but our BNDD headquarters failed to comply with the Department of State requirement to have us processed through its mandatory foreign orientation seminar, humorously known as charm school. As a result of this failure, we, the new arrivals, became the gossip among the stuffy diplomatic bureaucrats.

Regional Director Arpaio instructed us new agents and our wives to attend the U.S. Embassy newcomers welcoming party at the ambassador's residence. He told us to arrive at the ambassador's residence ten minutes before 7:00 p.m. and to go easy on the cocktails.

That evening the other new agents and their wives made a pit stop at my apartment, where we had a couple of drinks to calm our nerves regarding our first diplomatic party. We drove and parked near the ambassador's residence on Paseo De La Reforma Avenue and joined the other newcomers entering the ambassador's gated property. The ambassador and his staff were up front, greeting the newcomers as they entered.

I led our group, and when approaching the ambassador, we shook hands as I identified myself. "Good evening, Mr. Ambassador, my name is Arthur Sedillo."

After an uncomfortable silence, one of his flunkies asked me, "Who are you with?"

I smiled and responded, "I'm with my wife, Mariana Sedillo."

The ambassador's stone face almost cracked a smile, as he permitted me to go on to the other dignitaries in the welcoming committee line.

The correct answer was that I was with the Bureau of Narcotics and Dangerous Drugs, but I thought why not a bit of humor.

My wife Mariana found out that the woman's dress code was supposed to be a simple black dress with little if any jewelry. Since none of our agents' household goods had arrived, the wives' wardrobes were limited. Mariana wore a beautiful white summer dress, and she said she received several compliments tainted with sarcasm. I told her not to worry about it; she and the other agents' wives were a lot prettier than the snobby hags.

Eventually the embassy bureaucracy recognized that despite our lack of diplomacy, we were able to establish a better bilateral relationship with our counterparts because we leveled with them instead of bullshitting them with a smile.

On October 15, 1970, Regional Director Arpaio called me into his office as soon as I arrived. I made a quick mental check to see where I might have screwed up, knowing this was usually the only reason the "boss" called us into his office.

He said, "Art, I have some bad news. Last night your Miami Task Force Supervisor Hector Jordan was murdered."

My first reaction was that he was killed at his new post, Madrid, Spain, but Arpaio corrected me. "Actually he was murdered in his hometown. They were giving him a farewell party before his departure to Spain. A detective friend of his arrived a bit late, and he and Hector went back to the detective's car to get the forgotten farewell gift. They saw four thugs burglarizing the car and fought them, resulting in Hector's death. The detective was seriously injured."

CHAPTER 19

I thanked Arpaio for informing me, and I walked across the street to the Catholic church and said a prayer for our "*Por Que yo*" supervisor.

Finally our household goods arrived, and we moved to our permanent residence within the exclusive Colonia de Las Lomas area. When we approached our designated home, we were all in awe as we checked out the two-story cream stucco house with a reddish tile roof. A seven-foot wrought iron fence backed by a tall hedge enclosed the manicured lawn.

We walked into the house and noticed that the vast bay windows facing the left side provided a view of our beautifully landscaped yard. A fireplace was embedded in the corner of the living room, and the house had an ample dining room and kitchen. The upstairs had a den and four bedrooms with balconies at both ends of the hall.

Once we were settled, we registered the girls and Andrew in school. Gino was not happy seeing his older brother and buddy leaving him home for one more year.

A few days later on a lazy weekend, after having breakfast, Mariana and the girls planned a day by themselves and went shopping. The boys and I jumped on the sofa to watch an American football game.

Andrew got up and, without asking permission, picked up the telephone and dialed a phone number for the first time in his life. He asked whoever answered if he could talk to his friend John. After chit-chatting for a while, he turned around and asked me, "Dad, can John come and spend the night with us to play in our make-believe camp?" He was referring to the camping scene he and Gino had set up in their bedroom.

I told him that if his parents approved, it was okay with me. He returned to the phone and relayed my comment and then said to me that John's father wanted to talk to me to confirm the invitation.

John's father got on the phone and introduced himself as David Romero and that he was a Chicano from the Los Angles, California, area. I confirmed John's invitation, and David said he would bring him in a while.

DON'T EXPECT ANYTHING

I picked up Andrew and whirled him around, congratulating him on making his first phone call. I also thought that by the graciousness of David's conversation, it would be fun for me to make friends with a fellow Chicano not associated with the embassy.

Within fifteen minutes David and John arrived, and after exchanging greetings, John ran with the boys upstairs to their room, and I talked David into watching the football game with me. I fixed us a Bloody Mary, and we sat down and enjoyed the remainder of the game.

David told me he worked for some American corporation, without going into detail. I told him that I was a minor American bureaucrat in the U.S. Embassy.

I told him that Mariana and the girls were out shopping but that I would like to invite him and his wife to join us for supper. He told me his wife was in Los Angeles, but he would be glad to join us once I confirmed it with Mariana. I told him, "No problem; I'm sure she will agree."

Before he left, I took him upstairs so he could see the camp the boys had made.

I noticed David stared at my law enforcement plaques on the den wall, and I thought he appeared a bit nervous. I walked with him outside, and he agreed to return for supper.

When Mariana and the girls got home, I explained how Andrew had made his first phone call, explaining the presence of his friend John and that his father would be joining us for supper at seven.

Then I told her, "Honey, I enjoyed this guy's company and saw him as a potential Chicano friend; however, I'm a bit concerned that when we went upstairs to show him the kid's room, he glanced at my police diplomas, and he appeared to be a bit nervous. I think I should go to the embassy and do a quick check on him."

She agreed.

I rushed to the embassy and checked the NADDIS microfiche file and found a file identifying a David Romero from Los Angeles, California, as a heroin trafficker and BNDD fugitive. The physical description of the suspect further described him as having the tip portion of his left-hand middle finger amputated.

I telephoned Regional Director Arpaio, opening my conversation with the then-recent Sidney Poitier movie, "Guess who's coming to dinner." I told him that I suspected that I might have unwittingly invited a BNDD fugitive to dinner.

He instructed me, "Once you confirm that his fingertip is missing, talk to him alone and attempt to flip him as an informant. Tell him your house is surrounded by agents standing by for your call, if need be."

"Will do, sir."

I explained to Mariana about my findings and conversation with Regional Director Arpaio. I added, "Tonight I want you to act normal, and don't panic. After supper and once I have confirmed the amputation, you and the kids will excuse yourselves and go upstairs, and I will talk to him. Don't worry; I will discreetly check him out when he arrives to confirm that he is not armed."

David arrived just before seven carrying an expensive bottle of wine and a bouquet of flowers for Mariana. After I introduced him to Mariana and the girls, we all sat down and had an excellent supper.

Up to the dessert time, we noticed that David kept his left hand out of sight. Mariana, who was not known for her patience, asked him, "David, what time is it? I don't want to miss our TV telenovela."

I kind of panicked, seeing that the big clock on the wall showed the exact time. "Nice going, Mariana!" I would kid her later on. God bless my brilliant wife, because David raised his left hand to see his wristwatch. He told us it was five minutes to eight, and Mariana and I noticed his chopped finger. She quickly got up and told the kids to join her upstairs.

I invited David into our living room and sat by the fireplace and handed him a glass of his wine. I told him, "David, I know who you are, and I lied to you about being an embassy pencil pusher. I'm a BNDD agent and know you are a fugitive, and right now several of our agents are surrounding the house. The reason I'm not busting your ass is that I don't want this to be a traumatic experience for your wonderful son. Do you understand?"

Tears dribbled down his cheeks and his hands shook. He said, "What can I say? My own son brought me to the lion's mouth."

I reached over and softly patted him on the shoulder and said, "Look, David, we can do one of two things. We can have you arrested and extradited to the United States, or we can give you an opportunity to work off your beef and cooperate with us in identifying your Mexican source of heroin and help us set him up to be arrested and prosecuted here in Mexico. The choice is yours."

David didn't hesitate to assure me of his full cooperation, thanking me several times for giving him this option. I faked talking on my walkie-talkie to the agents, telling them that they could go home. David and I then discussed the relationship of our sons' friendship. David told me he would send his wife and son home so he would not endanger them while he is helping me.

At first, David provided general information that was already known to us, but I noticed that his efforts were less than what we desired.

After a few weeks of nonproduction, I pressured David, but with negative results. On a Sunday morning after returning from Mass, I found an envelope that had been pushed under our wrought-iron gate.

It was from David Romero, and it stated, "Dear Art, by the time you read this letter, my family and I are long gone from Mexico. For reasons you are familiar with, I can't tell you my new location, but the least I can do for you, in appreciation for the kindness you and your family displayed to my son, I want to warn you to be careful with MFJP First Commander Arturo Durazo Moreno.

"When you and I first met, I failed to tell you that once I learned you were an American narcotics agent, I told Commander Durazo, who in turn ordered me to become a counterspy and keep him informed of whatever you guys were doing. Be very careful with this man. He is very dangerous, and he told me that if he ever learns that you guys are investigating him, he will have you killed. When he told me that, I knew it was time to tip you off and for my family and me get the hell out of Mexico. God bless, David."

For whatever it was worth, because of the last bit of information David provided in his farewell letter, I made an official report documenting First Commander Arturo Durazo Moreno as a corrupt and dangerous official. The memorandum was classified as secret but was downgraded to unclassified years later, after he was declared a major criminal by the Mexican attorney general's office.

It should be known that Durazo resigned from the Mexican Federal Judicial Police and became the Mexico City chief of police. He continued his criminal and corrupt practices, becoming a millionaire. Among his many expenditures, he duplicated the Parthenon on one of his several properties. He was subsequently arrested in Puerto Rico and extradited back to Mexico, where he was imprisoned.

CHAPTER 20

OUR FIVE-YEAR-OLD SON Gino became sick with Still's disease and was evacuated to the San Antonio, Texas, Military Brooks Medical Center, accompanied by Mariana.

After a few days, Regional Director Arpaio showed his rare humanitarian side and called me into his office and said, "Art, I want you to go to the San Antonio, Texas, area to check out the area for future potential undercover assignments. Don't go near our office. Instead check out the Brooks Hospital area. Get it?"

"Yes, sir."

"Once you get there, relieve your wife so she can come back and take care of your other kids."

Lots of agents had bad-mouthed the boss, but as far as I was concerned, and especially after this gesture, in my book he was the best.

When I went to San Antonio to relieve Mariana, Gino told us, "When I grow up, I'm going to become a doctor." Both he and his older brother Andrew became eminent doctors.

One of the few domestic luxuries provided by our U.S. embassy was the commissary that imports stateside goodies not available on the local market. Mariana picked up a turkey, cranberry sauce, and marshmallows for our Thanksgiving dinner.

While she prepared dinner, I watched an American football game on TV, when my dear friend MFJP Agent Francisco Benavidez telephoned me. "Shit, I came to your embassy, and the guard told me that you Americans are celebrating some damn Thanksgiving Day."

"That's right. Don't you guys have a Thanksgiving Day?"

"Shit no, we don't have anything to be thankful for. Look, I don't want to mess up your holiday, but I have some critical information about Chilean cocaine traffickers smuggling their shit through our Veracruz seaport. This friend of mine is here only for a few hours before he leaves, and I wanted to introduce you to him. He is willing to help you bust these bastards."

"Man, the mere fact that you mentioned Chileans got my attention. They are currently our top priority target."

"Good. Get your ass down here to the Sanborn Café next to your office. We will be waiting for you."

"Brother, I'll be down there in fifteen minutes."

Mariana overheard my conversation and told me, "Get down there and back. Dinner will be ready in a couple of hours."

I met Francisco and his friend Prudencio (alias), who was a bodyguard for a millionaire. He told me, "My boss's son is a stupid shit that almost died from an overdose of cocaine. His father wanted me to find the dope pusher and kill him. Of course I told him I couldn't do that; I would have him arrested. Francisco told me that you would be able to set this guy up to be arrested. Can you do that? If at all possible, have him busted in the United States, because if they bust him here, they will probably cut him loose in a short time on a payoff."

"No problem, provided you give me enough details."

"I will not only give you the information you need, but I can also introduce you to a guy named Tano who owns a seafood place in Veracruz. He can introduce you to the Chilean trafficker named Chencho Dias, who works on a Chilean ship named *Lata*.

"Tano is a nice black guy that I have known since our childhood. Unfortunately he has fallen into those dopers' trap and helps set up clients for them in exchange for a small commission. Tano's Café is a hole in the wall half a block from where the ship docks."

After taking notes, Prudencio told me that after we finished talking he would be on his way to Veracruz and wanted to know when I would be able to join him there to introduce me to Tano.

I told Prudencio, "I'll be there this Saturday. What hotel do you recommend for me? I will probably need two adjoining rooms for my fellow agents, who will be conducting surveillance."

"No problem. I know the manager of the Emporia Hotel that is half a block from Tano's Café and is on the side of the boardwalk right in front of the dock where all the ships dock. I will get you two rooms that face the dock so you can check out the ship without a problem."

I rushed home to celebrate Thanksgiving dinner and to telephone Regional Director Arpaio, who authorized me to pursue the investigation, instructing me to get agents Moreno and Waddell to accompany me.

On Saturday morning the three of us drove to Veracruz, Mexico, stopping only at the Orizaba Tecate brewery, where we picked up a case of beer.

Prudencio was standing by for us in the hotel lobby and accompanied us to the two top-story connecting rooms with balconies and a view of the docking pier. Prudencio told us that he had checked with a contact and learned that the *Lajta* would be arriving that night.

After checking into the room and getting a bucket of ice for the beer that we placed in the bathtub, Prudencio and I walked half a block down the street to Tano's Seafood Café. Several feet before approaching the place we could hear the calypso music blaring out of the café juke's box. When we entered, Tano spotted us and came out dancing from behind the counter and greeted Prudencio with a hug, telling him, "My dear Prudencio, where in the hell have you been, brother? Its ages I haven't seen you." Tano was a black male about thirty-five years old.

He was wearing white shorts and a loud Hawaiian shirt protected by a black apron.

Prudencio responded, "I have to work for a living and don't have the luxury of not doing shit like you, brother."

Tano said, "What do you mean? I work like a Negro for just a few pesos a day."

Prudencio introduced me. "Look, Tano, I want you to meet a dear friend of mine, Arturo Chavez. He is a Chicano from Albuquerque, New Mexico."

Tano led us to a booth and insisted that we start with a Tecate beer and a shrimp cocktail, to be followed by a red snapper dinner.

He returned to the kitchen, placed our order, and then joined us.

Prudencio told him, "Look, brother, the reason we came to see you is that some time ago Arturo bought some cocaine from some damn Chilean, but after the delivery, he learned that the shit he got was not as good as the sample."

Tano interrupted Prudencio. "Brother, you need to say no more. There are lots of those crooked guys that keep ripping off clients. Now I don't want to stick my nose in your business, but since you have confided in me, I can resolve your problem."

Prudencio said, "That is why we are talking to you, *pendejo*. I told Arturo you would be able to give us some sound advice."

"I can do more than that. I have several good Chilean contacts, and I have introduced them to several clients that have never complained about the merchandise. If you want, I can introduce Arturo to an excellent connection that as a matter of fact should be arriving this evening."

I popped into the conversation. "Gee, Tano. That would be great. I want you to know that I'm interested in buying several kilograms, and I want them delivered in the United States. If the deal works out, I'm willing to pay you a good commission for your introduction to your connection."

Tano said, "As I said, say no more. My connection is no 'pinche' (ship dishwasher or less). He is a man of his word. I do know that after this port they continue to the United States, but do not know to which port."

We agreed that I would check with Tano later in the evening to see if Chencho arrived. Prudencio told Tano, "Brother, I knew you would not let us down. Unfortunately I have to return to Mexico City to my job."

Again, using his burned-out expression, Tano said. "Say no more, brother. I will take care of Arturo." We bid him farewell, and I left him a ten dollar tip.

Back in the hotel room, my two partners were relaxing on the balcony drinking beer and enjoying the sea breeze while checking for the arrival of the *Laja*.

I briefed them on my undercover contact with Tano and suggested that they go to the restaurant so they could eat and at the same time identify Tano.

As they departed, Waddell told me, "Get some more ice for the beer. It's going to be a long night."

At 11:30 the *Laja* arrived and docked right in front of us, about the distance of a football field away. Using binoculars we had a clear view of the crew mopping the deck and other clean-up duties. At about 12:30, some of the crew disembarked.

I walked down to Tano's while my surveillance team walked out in the general area, since returning to the small café shortly after eating there would look suspicious.

Tano saw me coming in, and playing the role that we were old friends, danced toward me in tune to the music, gave me a strong hug, and in a loud voice said, "My dear Arturo, long time no see. I kept waiting for you, thinking that you would be arriving a lot earlier. Where in the hell have you been?"

I responded, "Blame damn Mexicana Airlines. I got stuck in the Mexico City airport four hours because of flight delays. Anyway, I'm here, amigo."

He then whispered, "You got here just in time. The man was getting a bit impatient waiting for you."

He led me to the corner table and introduced me to Don Chencho, a man in his late forties, clean shaven, with a well-trimmed haircut. Tano excused himself, and I sat down across from Chencho.

I told him, "Don Chencho, please don't think that I'm abusive, but the only reason I agreed to talk to you was because of Tano's recommendation. I already have my connection for cocaine, but of course I'm always looking for a better deal."

He smiled and said, "I take no offense since I'm only talking to you because of the same referral. I can also assure you that the purity of my merchandise exceeds my competitors'. The minimum purity of my stuff is in the eighty-fifth percentile."

"That certainly gets my attention. I'm interested in making purchases of five to ten kilograms on each transaction. And I don't know if Tano told you, I want my merchandise delivered in the United States. I realized you will jack up the price for the delivery there, but as long as it is reasonable, I don't mind."

"Our next port is in Tampa, Florida. If you take it, here, it will cost you twenty-eight thousand dollars per kilogram. In Florida it will cost you thirty thousand dollars."

"Okay, I want ten kilograms, so that will cost me three-hundred-thousand dollars, correct?"

"That's it. Don Arturo, I have to tell you that I'm damn tired, and if it is all right with you, I would like to continue this conversation tomorrow. When we arrive at these foreign posts, after having worked all that day, we have to scrub the ship clean to pass inspection, so that means we have been working nonstop for close to fifteen hours."

"Damn, I don't blame you. Sure, I have no problem. Just tell me when and where you want to meet."

"Well, let's meet about ten in the morning, but I want to treat you to some of our famous Chilean wine, so we will go to the ship."

He paid his bill, and we walked out together. At the intersection of Paseo del Malecon and the actual pier, Bosse pointed to his ship and told me, "Look, let's meet right at this very spot at ten, and from here we'll go straight to the ship."

"Okay. *Hasta la vista*, Don Chencho."

The following morning I walked to the nearby Catholic Church, and after Mass had a hardy breakfast at La Parroquia Café. The specialty of that café was its coffee-milk. Waiters walked around carrying a metal pitcher and responded to customers banging their empty glasses with their spoons for refills.

Waddell and Moreno didn't take any chances and remained in their room and ordered their breakfast to their balcony, from which location they had me directly under observation.

Waddell told me, "Look, Art, we don't want to take any chances with you going aboard their ship, so I want to give you some additional assurance. Once you go aboard, have Chencho walk you to this side of the ship. Take your binoculars with you and hang them around your neck like the rest of the tourists. Once you are within view of the hotel, hand the binoculars to Chencho and tell him to look in our direction. I will be aiming my rifle and looking at him through the rifle scope. Before he shits his pants, just tell him that you are not alone and that we are your security team."

"That's a good idea. Just keep your fingers crossed that it will not spook him."

When I got to the designated corner, Chencho was already leaning on the building wall and picking his teeth with a toothpick. Agent Waddell took a photograph of the meeting. He told me that I looked more like the crook than Chencho. (2)

I apologized. "*Hola, amigo*, sorry for being a bit late. I overslept."

He said, "The fact that you have the luxury of oversleeping is a blessing and a sign that you have no worries."

"Besides being the big boss on your ship, you are also a philosopher?"

We laughed, and he escorted me to the ship. We walked through the gated entrance, and the Mexican Customs official just waved us through, barely raising his view from the newspaper he was reading.

CHAPTER 20

Once we were aboard, Chencho cautioned me to be careful not to slip on the recently scrubbed deck. When we got to the port side, I asked him to stop and handed him my binoculars and told him, "I want you to check out those two guys on that top balcony of that hotel."

He checked out the guys and dropped the binoculars and yelled at me, "What the hell is going on? They are pointing a rifle in our direction!"

"Don't panic, Chencho. As long as nothing happens to me, nothing will happen to you. You must understand that in this business it is important to have the needed security when conducting business. Those guys are my partners and bodyguards."

Chencho told me, "I don't want any trouble. If you don't trust me here, you can walk right off this ship, and we can forget all about doing business."

He handed me the binoculars, and I told him,

"Come on, Chencho, try walking in my shoes." I'm doing business in a foreign country with a third-country national. I'm just covering my ass. Wouldn't you do the same thing if you were me?"

His stern face finally broke into a smile, and he said, "I guess you're right." We both waved our hands at the agents, letting them know that everything was okay; and then, Chencho and I walked to the dining room.

He took a leather wine bag from a cooler and filled two plastic glasses. We made a toast that we would have a long and profitable friendship. He took out a small plastic bag from his shirt and handed it to me.

He said. "So you can see that I'm not playing games, this is a sample of the same material that will be contained in the ten kilograms I will deliver to you at Tampa. We will be arriving in Tampa on or about December the eighth."

"Okay, I will make sure to be there. Now needless to say that I will not be able to go on board because the U.S. Customs is not as casual as that Mexican Customs guy that waved us aboard. How do you want to make the transaction?"

"Now listen to me carefully. You want to meet me and my people at Joe's Bar's parking lot about three blocks from where we dock. You will not have a hard time locating it. I don't know or trust anyone in that bar, but we have found it a convenient place to do business in the bar parking lot. What you want to do is check every three hours starting at nine a.m., then noon, three p.m., and so forth. We will be there on one of those. Do you have any questions?"

"Yes, maybe a couple. First, will you make a one-time delivery with all ten kilos, or will it be broken up into smaller portions? I need to know because I will pay only for what is delivered at the time."

"Good question. I have two guys besides myself, and each of us can smuggle only two kilos body-wrapped, so we will have to make two trips, so we will deliver six on the first trip and four on the second trip. Oh. One more thing. I will go alone first and meet with you outside the bar so you can show me that you have the money. No offense intended, but you know, business is business."

"No problems. I will show you a substantial amount corresponding to the number of kilos you deliver."

"Fine. Do you have any other questions?"

"Just one. This is not directly related to our transaction, but taking advantage of your expertise on ships and so forth, I would appreciate your opinion. We are moving the merchandise from Tampa up the Gulf of Mexico to Houston, Texas, in a small yacht. Can you tell me where it would be best to hide the stuff?"

"Well, I don't know about yachts, but we hide ours behind the walls of our private quarters."

The smart ass just blew it. This was the information I needed to pass on to U.S. Customs.

I thanked Chencho and walked off the ship, agreeing to meet with him on or about December 8, 1970, in Tampa.

On December 7, 1970, I arrived in Tampa, Florida, and was happy to see my friend Agent Octavio Gonzales standing by for me at the airport baggage section. He had driven up from Miami to work with me in an undercover capacity.

He and I met with U.S. Customs supervisor Sam Johnson and Agent Paxson. I gave them a copy of suspect Chencho's photograph. We agreed that since the Customs officials now had the photograph of Chencho, we would change our arrest strategy from a buy-and-bust situation to a Custom's search-and-arrest case. By taking this action, I would be able to return to the Veracruz, Mexico, seaport and continue working in my undercover capacity, targeting other Chilean cocaine traffickers through Tano.

On December 8, Agent Gonzales and I waved Chencho down when he approached the parking lot at Joe's bar and had him join us. I introduced Octavio to Chencho telling him that he was my associate. I wanted Chencho to know Octavio in the event that I would not be available for future transactions.

Just to confirm his delivery, I quickly flashed him my opened brief-case displaying several stacks of twenty-dollar bills. Upon seeing the money, he licked his lips.

Once he left, we notified the U.S. Customs agents, who were also conducting a discreet surveillance of Chencho. I knew it would be the last time I would see him unless it became essential that I testify against him in the trial.

When Chencho returned to the ship, U.S. Customs Agents searched his quarters shared with Julio Segundo Herrera. Customs found and seized sixteen kilograms of cocaine. Both, Chencho, whose complete name is Chencho Gomez, and Herrera were arrested. They were subsequently prosecuted and imprisoned for several years.

Two weeks later on a Saturday, I received a telephone call from Prudencio, who told me that Tano had another Chilean client ready for me. Being that it was a weekend, I knew all the agents were out of town or on other assignments, but Regional Director Joe Arpaio told me, "Shit, Art, it's been a long time since I've worked undercover, so

I'll go with you."

I picked him up at his residence, and we drove to Veracruz. He telephoned MFJP National Director General Arriaga, who had authorized the bilateral investigation and would have the MFJP Veracruz agents standing by to assist us.

At Veracruz, we checked into two joining rooms at the Hotel Veracruz. We met with the MFJP agents and worked out the details of our undercover investigation.

It should be known that working undercover in Mexico is considered illegal entrapment; therefore, each time I worked in that capacity, the MFJP agents would tell the arrested suspects that I had escaped, been shot, or extradited.

Later in the evening Regional Director Arpaio and I walked into Tano's café where he greeted both of us in his usual dancing and hugging manner.

I introduced him to Arpaio as my Mafia boss named Josip Marcello.

Arpaio, with a unlit cigar sticking out of the side of his mouth, broke into a half smile and shook Tano's hand, saying, *"Buonasera, Signore."*

Tano was impressed and led us to a table occupied by Chilean suspects Bernardo Araya and Mario Herrera, and we exchanged greetings and introductions.

I ordered five kilograms of cocaine to be sold to us at $28,000.00 (U.S. currency) per kilo. It was agreed that they would deliver the five kilograms on the following morning at 9:00 a.m. at the Hotel Veracruz.

Bernardo told us that two other guys would be accompanying them, because each would have a kilogram and a fraction to complete the five kilograms. The cocaine would be body-wrapped.

The following morning Chileans Bernardo Araya, Mario Herrera, Jorge Pinochet, and Dionisio arrived at the hotel, and the MFJP agents arrested them when they exited the second floor elevator. After they were arrested and the five kilograms were removed from their bodies, the commander ordered two of his men, "Okay, you guys, now go and arrest the two gringos that were going to buy this shit."

I told the federales that if they could further pursue this investigation with Mexican Customs, they would probably find additional cocaine hidden behind the walls in the suspect's compartments. An additional fourteen kilograms were found and seized.

As a result of this investigation, the MFJP commander asked me for additional assistance in other drug-related investigations. I assigned my loyal informant Jorge to assist the Veracruz MFJP office, which resulted in several other successful drug-related investigations.

In Guadalajara, Mexico Agent in Charge Tom Zepeda picked me up at the airport regarding an undercover investigation. I would finally see the office I had helped create as a result of my participation with our national director Harry Giordano and the Mexican Federal Judicial Police at the Long Beach, California, FBN/State Police Seminar.

Unfortunately it didn't happen. Upon my arrival in Guadalajara, the local agents took me to a hotel where I was introduced to an informant. The informant took me to the house of major trafficker, aka Guerrero, who had recently been murdered, but his wife Manuela continued selling heroin.

When we entered the suspect's house, her bodyguards searched me to make sure I was not armed and then escorted the informant and me to their conference room. Dona Manuela, still dressed in black in honor of her husband's death, apologized for having me searched, but explained that since her husband's murder, she was taking all the necessary precautions.

I told her, "Madam, I don't blame you, and please accept my condolences. Jose (the informant) told me of your husband's tragic death."

She accepted my condolences and we got down to business. I told her that I wanted to purchase ten kilograms of heroin. She was selling a kilogram at $30,000. I told her I had the money at the hotel and was willing to make the transaction at her earliest convenience. She told me she would have to send her people for the heroin and would have it at the residence at 3:00 p.m. We finished the tequila margaritas she had

DON'T EXPECT ANYTHING

prepared for us and departed.

I told the BNDD/MFJP team to keep an eye on the suspect's people, because they would be going someplace for the ten kilograms. The team followed the bodyguards to a chicken ranch where they picked up the ten kilograms of heroin and were arrested, with the follow-up arrest of Dona Manuela. A picture of the ten kilograms were subsequently released in the local newspaper. (3)

I was quickly taken to the airport and returned to Mexico City, missing the opportunity to see the BNDD U.S. Consulate Guadalajara office.

CHAPTER 21

ON MARCH 23, 1972, our fifth child was born in Mexico City, making that day another of the happiest in my life. Since he was born under the U.S. Embassy jurisdiction, his citizenship was never in question. We named him Emiliano Francisco Sedillo as a tribute to Mexico revolutionary heroes Emiliano Zapata and Francisco {Pancho) Villa.

On April 27, 1972, our office, in coordination with the Mexican attorney general's task force, were conducting surveillance of French Corsican international drug trafficker Lucian Sarti. He was hiding in a residence in the exclusive Polanco Mexico City area. Sarti attempted to escape when we located him. He came out of the house shooting at us with a semiautomatic pistol. We returned fire and killed him.

Much has been said about Sarti, including the French *Le Mondo* newspaper that stated that Sarti was associated with Nazi collaborator Auguste Joseph Record. This source alleged that the criminal association may have been involved in the assassination of U.S. President John F. Kennedy.

This source also stated that when Sarti was killed in Mexico City, it was not reported in the United States. *Le Mondo* reported that Sarti's death was the result of a "close Mafia-police-Narcotics Bureau collaboration" in the United States to "shatter Corsican influence in the worldwide narcotics traffic and create a virtual monopoly of the U.S. Italian Mafia connection," whose key figure was Santo Trafficante.

These sources to *Le Mondo* were in part bullshit, because as stated, both the Mexican attorney general's task force and DEA agents were involved in the investigation, and the shootout with Sarti was reported to our respective governments. And most important, none of the law enforcement effort was in collaboration with a criminal element.

After Sarti's death, additional French Corsican associates were arrested in Mexico City, and I accompanied French authorities on the first leg of the flight from Mexico City to Miami, Florida, from which location the French authorities and suspects continued to France.

Moments after the Sarti shootout, Mexican Attorney General Ojeda Palladia asked to interview all of us who had been involved in the incident. Special Task Force Attorney General's Commander Florentino Ventura insisted that I accompany his team to the attorney general's meeting. Attorney General Palladia asked me, "Did you participate in the shooting incident?"

I knew it was a sensitive issue and deliberated for a short while until I saw Commander Ventura nod his head in the affirmative before I responded, "Sir, I did shoot in defense of my fellow MFJP agents, and if I violated our diplomatic relationship, I know I may be expelled, but I will always respond to the defense of our fellow agents."

The attorney general was silent for a while and then extended a handshake told me, "Long live our bilateral relationship."

The Mexico City Italian Mafia representative Josip "Pino" Catania owned a shirt shop a block from the U.S. Embassy at 153 Hamburgo Street. He was in his mid to late thirties; about five feet, six inches tall; and weighed about a hundred fifty pounds. He dressed mostly in fancy dress shirts with the sleeves slightly rolled up, displaying an expensive Rolex watch to complement his large diamond rings.

Since arriving in Mexico City, I had become aware of Catania and had been conducting surveillance on his activities. He usually had breakfast around ten in the morning at the nearby Danny's Restaurant. I made it a point to pop into that place so that the suspect would think that I was probably a local low-level employee on my coffee break.

On one occasion he even asked me for a match to light his cigarette. From that day on we sometimes acknowledged each other's presences with a courtesy hand wave, greeting without conversing.

To make sure that I would not miss the stateside and Canadian Mafia visitors, Arpaio approved that I get a room at the Hotel Presidente that was on Humburgo Street less than a hundred yards from Catania's shirt shop. I was able to get a room on the fourth-floor corner, from which, with the aid of binoculars, I had a perfect view right into Catania's shirt shop. I could see him sitting in his leather chair with his feet propped up on his desk as he read the newspaper and picked his nose.

After I spent several days in the hotel, one of the agents tipped me off that Arpaio was concerned about my prolonged stay in the hotel room and was sending Agent Waddell to check me out.

To show them how much I was suffering, I had the hotel clerk, which I had befriended, bring me a steak dinner and set up the mini table with a candle and a bowl of pink roses. The clerk went a step further and brought the violin player from the hotel mariachi group to play when my visitor arrived.

When Agent Waddell knocked on the door, I told him to come in as the violinist played "Malaguena" while I sat and enjoyed my steak and glass of wine.

Agent Waddell got a kick out of my charade, and they never bothered me for the rest of the surveillance.

When we learned that the visiting Mafia group was on its way to Acapulco, New York Agent Ron Provencher and I discreetly conducted surveillance of the suspects on their flight to Acapulco.

At the Acapulco Hotel, I was able to conduct surveillance on the Mafia suspects at the poolside and at different nightclubs they

DON'T EXPECT ANYTHING

frequented. Unfortunately for Agent Provencher, he had to maintain a low profile, since his hotel room was adjacent to the suspects' room and his job was to try to overhear their conversations.

Every once in a while I would lie back on a pool lounge chair wearing my straw hat and sunglasses. I could see Agent Proventure peeping down at the suspects and me from his open room window. I would discreetly raise my coconut cocktail and toast him.

He, in turn, would extend his middle finger to me.

During one short break when the suspects went on a two-day cruise, I rushed to Mexico City, and when I submitted my voucher without receipts for drinks, Regional Director Arpaio chewed my ass out, telling me the next voucher had better have proof of the drinks I consumed. I argued with him there was no way I was going to ask for a receipt while conducting surveillance on the dangerous Mafioso guys.

He told me, "Figure out something, but have proof next voucher, or drink water."

I returned to Acapulco for five additional days until the Mafia suspects returned to the United States and Canada.

I prepared the bulkiest expense voucher ever. I retained the swizzle sticks that came with each cocktail I had consumed, stapled them to sheets of paper, and attached them to the voucher.

When I placed my bulky voucher in Arpaio's inbox, several of us peeked to see his reaction. When he picked it up, he appeared to be pissed but then broke into a rare smile. He came out, and all he told me was, "Very funny, Sedillo."

As a result of my surveillance on Catania and others, I testified against him and other suspects in the Eastern New York City Judicial District under the direction of Assistant U.S. Attorney Thomas Puccio.

When Josip Catania saw me testify against him and his associates, he almost shit his pants to learn that I was a U.S. Federal Narcotics Agent and not a Mexican subordinate store clerk. He and his associates were found guilty of illicit drug trafficking and organized criminal activities and were imprisoned for several years.

CHAPTER 21

New York Times reporter Morris Kalan reported Catania's trafficking on August 22, 1973, as follows:

ALIEN HELD AS KEY TO HEROIN TRAFFIC

An Italian haberdasher from Mexico City was charged in a Federal indictment unsealed in Brooklyn yesterday with being the pivotal figure in the flow of $132 million worth of heroin from France to major dealers in the United States and Canada.

The 39-year-old suspect, Giuseppe (Pino) Catania, a native of Palermo, Sicily, had operated a fashionable custom-shirt business near the American Embassy in Mexico City since 1962. Under the name of Le Due Shirt Shop at 153 Hamburgo Street, the business prospered but not nearly as much, Federal officials contend, as his alleged trafficking in heroin from Marseilles.

Drug Enforcement Administration agents removed Mr. Catania at 11 p.m. Monday from an Air France jetliner at the Houston International Airport in Texas. Cooperating Mexican authorities had deported him as an undesirable alien in connection with charges that he had falsified his income taxes. The plane was bound for further stops in Paris and Rome.

United States Magistrate H. Lingo Platter set Catania's bail at $1 million. The defendant, who, was described as five feet six inches tall and weighing 145 pounds, lived with his wife and two children in Mexico City. Authorities said he would be taken to Brooklyn to plead to a conspiracy count.

In Washington, John R. Bartels, Jr., acting administrator of the Drug Enforcement Administration, called Mr. Catania one of the principal smugglers of heroin into this country. The indictment was reportedly the first of a major Mexican-based drug trafficker.

Mr. Catania's alleged operation was said to have flourished, despite reports more than two years ago that a campaign by the United States and Mexico to control drug traffic across their border appeared to have been effective. The campaign, known as Operation Cooperation followed the unsuccessful Operation Intercept that Washington initiated in late 1969 to curb the flow of narcotics from Mexico.

Drugs Shipped From France

Complaints about disruptions to traffic caused by Operation Intercept, in which 1,000 narcotics agents were assigned to border areas to search all persons entering the United States from Mexico, strained relations between the two countries for a time.

The indictments charges that between March, 1970 and January 31, 1972, Mr. Catania and three co-conspirators imported large quantities of heroin into the United States. In September 1971, a truck containing 110 pounds of the drug arrived at Kennedy International Airport from France for transshipment to Mexico City, the indictment said.

A total of 264 pounds were routed from Paris to Lima, Peru, then by private plane to Mexico City in December 1971, according to Thomas P. Puccio, an assistant United States attorney who is prosecuting the case.

Co-conspirators Named

Among those named as coconspirators but not defendants was Michel Nicoli, described as a major narcotics dealer in Europe, who is awaiting trial in a separate narcotics conspiracy indictment.

Also named was Carlo Zippo, under arrest in Naples and awaiting extradition to New York, where he is charged with Nicoli. A third alleged co-conspirator, Lucian Sarti, was shot and killed in Mexico City while resisting arrest in April 1972.

Associates of Sarti provided information pointing to Mr. Catania as a principal in the drug movement, according to Mr.

Bartels. Sarti was an associate of Auguste Ricard, who was convicted here as a key narcotics dealer.

Federal sources here said that the trail ended with Mr. Catania in Mexico City. They speculated that heroin shipments from there could have been by automobile, by private plane or by courier to various points in this country and to Montreal.

After the expulsion of Catania, I thought I was finished with the Mafia, when I was assigned again to Acapulco to conduct surveillance on Corsican Mafia suspects. These suspects were French from the Corsican Island near France but are more active in Marseilles, France. The main suspects we would be following were not located, but two other Corsican suspects, Antoine and Petro, befriended me at the Presidente Hotel bar.

The Mexican Attorney General's Special Team accompanied me on this operation. My Mexico City landlord, which I will not identify for security reasons, owned a nice apartment in Acapulco and permitted the attorney general's team and me to stay in it free of charge. The apartment had a nice swimming pool and a walled-in landscaped yard.

Upon meeting with Angelino, Petro, and a third Corsican, I lied and said that I was from the Acapulco area since childhood but currently resided in Mexico City. After a couple of margarita cocktails, Angelino came right out and asked me if by any chance I knew Josip Catania.

I became concerned that the suspects may have figured out who I was and were about to do me in or just leave me alone. I mentally debated for a short while before I answered and said, "Look, guys, it has been nice talking to you, but if I knew that guy, I would not tell you. Who in the hell are you, Interpol or something?"

They laughed and one of them said, "We can assure you that we are not associated with any police."

I changed the conversation, in part because of my limited French. I had a brainstorm and told the guys, "You know, tomorrow my friends are celebrating my birthday at my apartment. I would very much like to invite you. Nothing big, just a small group of us. Bring your swimsuits if you want to go swimming."

They agreed to attend, and I told them I would pick them in the lobby at 7:00 p.m.

I got a hold of my landlord who quickly organized a party and invited several of his Acapulco friends. He went overboard and decorated a chair elevated on the diving board. He told me, "Arturo, you will play the role of Don Arturo, the son of a very important Mexican gangster, and sit in this chair. My friends and your task force team will pay homage to you, making your guests think that you are the 'Big Honcho.'"

When I arrived with my two Corsican friends at the apartment, a mariachi group started playing the Mexican version of the Happy Birthday song and all those present sang in tune with the players.

My guests were welcomed with the traditional *abraso* (hug) and furnished with coconuts containing piña coladas.

The party couldn't have been more successful. The suspects opened up to me, telling me that they were interested in exchanging the famous Acapulco Gold Marijuana for heroin. They also invited me to visit them in Nice, France, where they owned a nightclub. I agreed to visit them, and then I escorted them to a taxi for them to return to their hotel. They claimed they could not stay longer because they had an early flight the following morning.

Back in Mexico City, I discussed my meeting with Regional Director Arpaio, telling him that the suspects might be associated with major violator Catania, and they had invited me to France to finalize plans in exchanging Acapulco Gold Marijuana for heroin. I told him that unfortunately the Mexican Feds were not able to positively identify the suspects after checking the Presidente Hotel and International Airport records.

The investigation was coordinated with DEA headquarters and our Paris, France, DEA regional office.

On June 17, 1974, I arrived in Paris, France, and met with our agents at the U.S. Embassy and their French counterparts and made sure that the suspects I was going to contact in Nice, France, were not associated with Lucian Sarti's associates, in whose expulsion I had been involved. These agents conducted surveillance on my meetings with the suspects in Nice, France.

The suspects instructed me to stay in the Prom des Angelis Hotel, insisting they would pay for my accommodations. I spent the first part of my night looking for bugs (concealed hearing devices). My first meeting with the suspects was at their nightclub, where they provided drinks at no cost. In this session we made tentative plans to meet the following day at the recreational beach right off the hotel where I was staying.

The following day they showed up and we continued making plans for exchanging tons of marijuana for kilos of heroin. During this meeting, they introduced me to a distinguished-looking man dressed in suit and tie. I found the introduction rather strange, in the sense that the man garbled his name, and our contact was most brief. When he walked off, I suspected that he was packing a pistol because of the bulge on the back of his hip concealed by his suit jacket.

In a follow-up meeting with our agents and French counterparts, I explained my meeting with the suspects and their well-dressed associate. Because of the total lack of knowledge of the suspect's identification and no additional intelligence tying these guys with the Mafia Corsican group, it was agreed that if the suspects didn't make contact with me within twenty-four hours, we would discontinue the investigation. The local authorities could subsequently positively identify the suspects to determine their involvement in illicit drug traffic. I did add that the possibility existed that the third person I had met may have been some kind of government agent, because Petro kept pushing me to smuggle the ton of marijuana, making me think that the guys might be informants. After the suspects failed to make contact with me, I returned to Mexico.

CHAPTER 22

IN THE EARLY 1970s Regional Director Joe Arpaio was the regional director covering the largest foreign jurisdiction, which included Mexico as well as Central and South America.

He told me, "Our Costa Rica U.S. ambassador, Vance Vaky, has requested our assistance in immobilizing several significant international cocaine traffickers that are using Costa Rica as a transshipment point to the United States. I'm sending you down there to check it out."

"Yes, sir, when will I be going and for how long?"

"Take off on Monday and pack clothing for a couple of weeks, but your time down there will be determined by the ambassador. Possibly you will be going down there more than once, so play it by ear."

I took a Braniff flight from Mexico City and arrived in San Jose, Costa Rica, in the evening. I was quickly processed through Customs, and a U.S. Embassy representative named Julio Garcia was standing outside the baggage area with my name printed on a board. We met, and after introductions, Luis told me he would be my day-to-day contact.

As we drove to the downtown area, I marveled at the beautiful tropical city. Luis gave me a preliminary briefing about my assignment.

After dropping off my suitcase at the hotel, we continued to the U.S. Embassy.

We had a meeting with Ambassador Vaky and his staff, and I was briefed on the international drug trafficking organizations using Costa Rica as a transshipment point between the source countries to the United States. The most prominent trafficker was Angel Coronel Del Toro, who worked for the notorious international cocaine trafficking organization headed by Adolfo Soboski Tobias, a Uruguayan national residing in Santiago, Chile, where the corrupt Allende regime allegedly protected him.

After the embassy meeting, Luis took me to meet Costa Rican Attorney General Rodrigo Araya Pacheco and his national police director.

The following morning Luis picked me up to introduce me to a special team that would be working with us. We drove to a restaurant near a downtown park. The owner, an elderly gentleman sitting behind the cash register, told us the team was standing by for us upstairs.

A thirtyish guy opened the door, introduced himself as Costa Rica Captain Carlos Hernandez Rambolt, escorted us in, and introduced me to his six-member team. I had a feeling that I had seen the guy previously and asked him about it. He smiled and said, "Yeah, I have the same feeling about you. Maybe we ran into each other in Miami during Operation Eagle. I was working with the company unit as a member of BUNCIN." (A CIA drug enforcement unit)

Carlos called the meeting to order and said, "Don Arturo, I want you to know that we are all professionals, and our mission is to protect you and assist you in any way possible while you are in this country."

"Number one, knock off the 'Don' (sir) title, since I don't have the age or prominent status to merit the title. I'm simply Arturo. Please consider me a fellow team member."

They all gave me a high five wave.

Carlos continued. "Coronel Del Toro and all his associates are a bunch of spineless cutthroats and are considered dangerous. We will not restrict your movements but strongly recommend that if you are not with Don Julio or our men, maintain a low profile."

"Thanks, Captain. I have a lovely wife and five kids and don't plan on leaving her a widow and the kids orphans. You can count on my full cooperation."

Carlos continued, "Our first target is fugitive Angel Coronel Del Toro. We have a general idea where he hangs out, but he is always on the move in and out of the country. He is very smart, and I'm sure he suspects we are on his trail. He always changes addresses and uses several aliases.

"Now that you are here we will intensify our efforts to locate him to extradite him to the States.

"On another priority, we have an informant named Javier who can introduce you to cocaine trafficker Galo Canessa, who pushes his shit for a major trafficker named Adolfo Soboski, who operates out of Santiago, Chile. Actually all these suspects are part of the Soboski organization."

The informant, Javier, was brought up from the downstairs café so we could meet and agree on our undercover story. It was decided that I would go to the same bar a couple of times alone and let it be known that I'm looking for Javier, who is supposed to meet me at that location. Eventually we meet there and set up the meeting with Canessa.

Carlos agreed to the idea and cautioned his men not to go into that place prematurely, fearing that they may be identified, but to conduct surveillance from the outside when I was in there.

After the meeting, I went to the bar. I found it to be an uppity place furnished with mahogany interior and thick rugs. The jukebox was playing soft classical and jazz music, further contributing to the ambiance. I told the bartender that I was from El Paso, Texas, and that I had made arrangements to meet my friend Javier at this location.

After a couple of these individual separate meetings, we finally met and made a big scene about our finally hooking up. Surprisingly and entirely unbeknown to us, in our third meeting, Javier saw suspect

Galo Canessa patronizing the same place without our having to set up the meeting with him. He was sitting at the other end of the bar, and it was he who saw and approached us.

Not only would I be able to initiate this substance case, but I would also develop an international conspiracy case against major violator Soboski.

Javier and Canessa greeted each other with a macho hug, and then I was introduced to him. Javier told Canessa, "Talking about weird circumstances, I have been looking for you for the past week to introduce you to my friend Arturo Chavez, but shit, you are one hard *hombre* to find."

Javier told Canessa that I was interested in purchasing cocaine. Canessa requested that we move to an isolated booth to speak in private.

In the booth, Canessa told me, "Shit, I saw you a couple of times here, but of course I didn't know who in the hell you were."

I admitted frequenting the place for the sole purpose of hooking up with Javier. We got down to business, and I agreed to purchase cocaine from him.

Canessa told me that I would not have to worry about smuggling the cocaine into the United States because his organization had the best smuggling devices.

We agreed to meet at the same place the following day. He agreed to sell me two canisters, each holding a quarter pound of cocaine, for $250.00 each. I told him that it would be only a sample buy, because I had intentions of purchasing multi-kilograms if the price and quality was good.

The following day I met Canessa at the same place, and he sold me two hair-spray canisters containing the cocaine. The top of the cylinder cans had been sealed off to contain a bit of hairspray in the event Customs officials or other authorities checked them out.

After the second delivery of four cans, Canessa was arrested, and we flipped him as an informant and had him telephone his intermediate source, Roberto Sucre Candon Reyes, in Ecuador. During the undercover phone call, Candon told us he would have his courier, a female named Norma Ordonez, deliver the three kilograms of cocaine we had ordered. All involved were subsequently arrested at the San Jose International Airport when the suspects attempted to smuggle the cocaine into the country. We made the operation appear that a smart Costa Rican Customs official had suspected the hairspray canisters containing the cocaine when he found them in the suspect's suitcase. He punched a hole on the lower end of one of the hairspray canisters, and the white power poured out. A total of four kilograms were located and seized in several hairspray containers.

Sometime after, I bought two more hairspray cans containing cocaine from suspect Ambrosio Gustavo Lopez. It was a buy/bust deal, in that we arrested all the associated suspects and recovered all of the $1,000.00, plus $310 from a previous purchase. An additional 662 grams of cocaine were also seized.

Several days later Carlos called me to come to the Boroca Café because Angel Coronel Del Toro, accompanied by two other guys, was at the café. Carlos wanted me to confirm the suspect's identification.

I had a recent photograph of Coronel Del Toro provided by our headquarters BNDD office. Luis dropped me off near the café, and I walked into the place and sat down two booths away from the suspects and confirmed Coronel Del Toro's identification.

Through the window, I gave Carlos a thumb's up signal, confirming that the suspect was Coronel Del Toro. Carlos and his team rushed in and arrested Coronel Del Toro and his two associates.

I noticed a young teenager with the team and asked Julio who the kid was. He told me he was Jose Maria Figueres, the son of President Pepe Figueres. Julio said, "He is a real gung-ho kid and is an honorary member of the national law enforcement agency.

A search of Coronel Del Toro's house was conducted, but no drugs were found. However, we found several incriminating documents, including Chilean and American suspects' names and addresses as well as several falsified passports.

CHAPTER 22

The Costa Rican Supreme Court heard Angel Segundo Coronel Del Toro's case and ordered him extradited to the United States.

On March 13, 1973, Ambassador Vince Vaky sent a cable to Washington, D.C., Department of State and BNDD headquarters that stated in part:

"WE ARE PLEASED TO CONFIRM THAT SUSPECT CORONEL DEL TORO DEPARTED THIS MORNING FOR MIAMI ON LACSA 620 PER REFTEL ACCOMPANIED BY COSTA RICAN ATTORNEY GENERAL ARAYA, JOSE MARIA FIGUERES, BNDD SPECIAL AGENT SEDILLO AND THREE OTHERS."

When my flight was in the air and approaching the Miami International Airport, a flight attendant approached me and told me, "Sir, please come with me. The pilot wants to talk to you." I followed her to the pilot's compartment, and he handed me his headphones and told me, "Don Arturo, a law enforcement official wants to speak to you."

I wondered who in the hell wanted to talk to me that couldn't wait until we landed. I spoke, "This is Agent Arthur Sedillo. Hello."

Miami Regional Director Benjamin Theisen, aka "The Bat-Man," identified himself and told me, "The top of the morning to you, Agent Sedillo, and congratulations on a job well done. Listen, the damn U.S. Customs wants to take credit for this arrest, so the moment that you guys touch ground, I want you to place Coronel Del Toro under arrest and Mirandize the shit out of him, okay?"

"Yes, sir. You got it. Nice talking to you."

When the plane touched down on the Miami International Airport tarmac, I quickly placed Del Toro under arrest and warned him of his Miranda rights. At the same time, a team of U.S. Customs agents rushed toward us. I saw BNDD Agent Pete Scrocca run toward them like an offensive football end, blocking the Customs agents. He was followed by Regional Director Theisen, who was smiling, knowing that I had already placed the suspect under arrest.

The Costa Rican team joined us at the U.S. Magistrate Court, where Del Toro was bonded over on half a million dollars.

We wined and dined the Costa Rican troops, including Costa Rican president's son Jose Maria Figueres, who by then had become my friend.

Several other significant cases were initiated during my several trips to Costa Rica

In my last case in Costa Rica, we flipped one of the defendants as an informant and had him place a telephone call to major violator Adolfo Soboski in Santiago, Chile, and negotiated for a multi-kilogram purchase of cocaine.

Even though Soboski agreed to the transaction, it never materialized, because of the 1973 Pinochet Chilean coup d'état in which hundreds of people, including Soboski were arrested and held on the football field. Soboski was extradited to Uruguay and on to the United States on conspiracy charges to smuggle large amounts of cocaine.

However, it should be noted that one of the conspiracy charges against Soboski was made as a result of my hairspray-can cocaine purchases made in Costa Rica. As reported in *Newsweek* December 17, 1973, page thirty-eight shows Soboski's photograph and states in part:

"It was a tale that made *The French Connection* seem like small change. For nine years, as U.S. Drug Enforcement Administration officials told the story last week, Adolfo Soboski Tobias, 50, a suave Uruguayan national living in Chile, presided over a massive cocaine-smuggling empire that grossed him a cool $20 million a year and flooded the U.S. with cocaine that topped $600 million in street value. In all, said one DEA intelligence officer, Soboski had shipped more cocaine into the country than any other single person, but authorities said they didn't even know of his existence until a can of VO5 hairspray blew his cover last fall.

"Sobieski's arrest capped a yearlong investigation by U.S. agents cooperating with police of five Latin American countries. It was a

CHAPTER 22

small-time dealer arrested last fall in New York who gave authorities their first lead; the dealer spoke vaguely of a Costa Rican gang that smuggled cocaine inside aerosol spray cans. The Bureau of Narcotics and Dangerous Drugs sent an undercover agent who worked his way into the gang by posing as a well-heeled 'American connection,' and in due course, the agent came up with an Alberto VO5 can containing a small amount of cocaine. But the Costa Rican gang, he reported, was just a small part of a much larger operation involving smugglers in Guatemala and Mexico and a Santiago businessman named Soboski."

After purchasing the hairspray cans in Costa Rica, I flipped the seller to become my informant and had him telephone Soboski in Santiago, Chile, to sell us a large amount of cocaine. However, right at that time, the Chilean Allende regime toppled, and Soboski lost his protection and was incarcerated with political prisoners in the stadium.

When he saw that some of these prisoners were being executed, Soboski paid a bribe to get out but was turned over to the Uruguayan Embassy in Santiago, Chile, who in turn returned him to Uruguay, where the local authorities and BNDD agents extradited him to the United States. I testified against him in New York.

Toward the end of my Costa Rican assignment, President Pepe Figueres's son, Jose Maria, came early in the morning to my hotel, and on behalf of his mother, First Lady Karen de Figueres invited me to come to their residence. I telephone Ambassador Vaky, who authorized my visit.

At the president's residence, First Lady Mrs. Figueres was most gracious, thanking me for my major contribution in immobilizing major drug traffickers from their country and for my assistance in causing the creation of their national drug enforcement agency, which turned out to be her initiative.

The Costa Rican National Narcotics Enforcement Agency was officially created, and the attorney general made me an honorary life member, which included issuing me official credentials. (5)

CHAPTER 23

ON MARCH 28, 1973, President Nixon submitted to Congress Reorganization Plan Number 2, merging BNDD (Bureau of Narcotics and Dangerous Drugs), ODALE (Office of Drug Abuse Law Enforcement), and a large contingent from U.S. Customs into a new 2,000-person agency named Drug Enforcement Administration (DEA).

Like in all reorganizations, heads rolled, mostly at the top management level. We peons and former FBN/BNDD agents could not have cared less and quickly gave our new organization's acronym our own meaning: DEA: "Don't Expect Anything." The moniker gave me the idea for titling this book with the same acronym.

The reason for this negative attitude among former FBN and BNDD agents was that as a result of the reorganization at the Washington, D.C., level, word was that the former U.S. Customs administrator and subsequent ODALE National Director Myles Ambrose was expected to become DEA's first national administrator. Most former FBN/BNDD supervisors were scheduled to be downgraded, because of the legendary FBN/U.S. Customs feud.

To confirm this probability, our national commissioner, Henry Giordano, was downgraded to assistant administrator before he retired.

Just before the reorganization was announced, the Costa Rican government and our U.S. ambassador in that country requested the opening of a BNDD (DEA) office in the Costa Rican U.S. Embassy. Our Regional Director Joe Arpaio, without hesitation, recommended that I be assigned to that post as its attaché, since I had initiated all the investigations in that country and had established a good working relationship with Ambassador Vaky and the Costa Rican officials up to the presidential level.

Up to that point I had been a happy camper, in the sense that my career had been a smooth operation with normal career advancements.

Unfortunately, before the official announcement for the Costa Rican post was confirmed, and as a direct result of the DEA reorganization, Myles Ambrose was calling the shots, even though as of yet he had not been appointed as its national director. He had our boss, Regional Director Joe Arpaio, shit canned to Phoenix, Arizona, because he heard that Arpaio did not permit the U.S. Customs attaché at the Mexico City U.S. Embassy to have contact with the Mexican attorney general and Federal Police.

Former U.S. Customs Supervisor Tom Dean became our new Mexico City DEA director. Three former U.S. Customs agents stationed in the Mexico City U.S. Embassy were transferred to our Mexico City DEA Office. As far as I was concerned, two of them, Lee Riggs and Horace Cavitt, were outstanding agents, but I would have problems with the third, named Bruce Van Mater.

It just so happened that once the reorganization took place, except for the confirmation of Myles Ambrose in the national director position, the Costa Rican DEA post was officially announced.

I was surprised that our new regional director, Dean, disregarded former Regional Director Arpaio's recommendations to assign me to that post. He, instead, sent Agent Van Matre to Costa Rica to evaluate the need to open that office. His evaluation, whether they liked it or

DON'T EXPECT ANYTHING

not, would have to be based entirely on my work at that post.

When Agent Van Mater returned from Costa Rica and agreed for the need to open that post, he solicited for the position, which Regional Director Dean immediately granted to him.

I argued for the post to no avail, but to somewhat pacify me, Regional Director Dean sent both Agent Van Mater and me to DEA headquarters to go before an alleged reviewing board to determine the selection to that post.

While on the commercial flight to headquarters, Van Meter told me in a smirking manner, "I hate to tell you, Art, but I already know that they are going to assign the post to me."

I responded, "If they are going to pick us based on our professional productivity at that post, you are fucked. But if your U.S. Customs rabbis that are taking over all the top management positions are calling the shots, you are probably right."

When we got to DEA headquarters, Chief of Latin American Operations Larry "Jerry"' Stickler, whom I considered a good person, tipped me off that the selection process was already rigged to give the position to Van Meter.

Seeing that the career board didn't have a complete hearing convinced me it was not interested in what I had to say. The board assigned the post to Agent Van Matre.

Back in Mexico City, I licked my wounds and hit the road, initiating more cases.

In mid 1974, I was assigned to make undercover contact with major cocaine international trafficker Kenneth Burnstine, a pilot and former U.S. Marine lieutenant colonel. The suspect was interested in making multi-kilogram cocaine and marijuana purchases.

To pursue this unique investigation, I would have to change my usual undercover persona from a buyer to a seller of multi-kilograms of cocaine and marijuana.

Burnstine used his aircraft to smuggle illicit drugs from foreign countries into the United States. Because of his refusal to negotiate with new clients, we had to initiate the rarely used reverse undercover technique in which the agent plays the role of the source of narcotics. Once the suspects agree to purchase drugs, they are charged with conspiracy to possess, smuggle, and buy narcotics for resale to U.S. clients. In this case, I would be portraying the role of a Mexican trafficker.

I telephoned Burnstine from my Mexico City undercover phone at home and made preliminary arrangements to meet him in Veracruz, Mexico.

He called me back in my absence, and my teenage daughter Athena disregarded my orders never to answer that phone. She answered it and had a short conversation with Burnstine.

After exchanging greetings and asking for me, Burnstine told Athena, "My dear, you speak English like an American." Athena answered him, "Of course. Don't you know that Mexico is on the North American continent?"

When I got home, Athena told me about the phone call, and after I reprimanded her, I telephoned Burnstine and made final arrangements to meet him at the Veracruz Hotel in Veracruz, Mexico. DEA Agent Ruben Salinas accompanied me to Veracruz, and we called Burnstine's hotel room and told him to come join us at the hotel café. When he showed up, he was accompanied by former American Airlines pilot Robert Charles Davison.

Upon seeing the second person, I acted annoyed and told Burnstine that I had agreed to meet with him and no one else. I said, "I don't know who in the hell this guy may be. For all I know, he could be a cop. Those damn narcos are all over the place."

Burnstine apologized and told Davison to wait for him in the hotel room. Davison immediately departed.

When we sat down, we chitchatted for a while and then got down to business. Burnstine ordered forty kilograms of cocaine and 500 kilograms of marijuana. We also talked about larger future transactions.

As we ate and talked, Burnstine kept complimenting my white Guayabera shirt. Finally I took it off and gave it to him. He, in turn,

DON'T EXPECT ANYTHING

gave me his sweaty yellow shirt. He put on my shirt, but I just folded his, since I was wearing a T-shirt.

Burnstine and Davison were subsequently arrested in Miami, Florida, and charged with conspiracy to smuggle drugs into the United States. Both Agent Salinas and I testified against them in Miami Federal Court.

During my testimony, the conversation Burnstine had with my daughter surfaced; he lowered his head in embarrassment as the judge and jury laughed when hearing Athena telling him that Mexico was in North America.

As a former U.S. Marine sergeant, I felt sad that such a high-ranking former Marine had involved himself in the dirty business of drug trafficking.

Sometime after, I was glad to hear that Burnstine became a government informant and implicated several significant traffickers. Unfortunately, before those suspects were arrested, Burnstine was killed in an air show when his aircraft failed to come out of a spin.

I suspected that the criminal element had murdered him, but according to the authorities, it was determined that because of the completely burned aircraft, no evidence of wrongdoing could be established.

CHAPTER 24

A RELIABLE SOURCE of information told me that an American Brooklyn trafficker named Murray Kessler had weapons he wanted to trade for heroin. Kessler's associate was Richmond Harper, who owned a ranch on the Texas-Mexico border.

I coordinated the investigation with U.S. Customs undercover agent Cesar Diosdado, who traveled to Mexico City, and I put him in touch with my source.

Agent Diosdado, in his undercover capacity, subsequently met Harper at Eagle Pass, Texas. Harper in turn placed Diosdado in touch with suspect Murray Kessler in New Jersey.

The DEA Brooklyn Organized Crime Strike Force assisted Agent Diosdado in a sting operation that resulted in the suspects selling explosives for a million dollars, at which time all the suspects were arrested and the explosives seized.

On November 10, 1972, *New York Times* reporter Martin Torchon released a lengthy story regarding Miles J. Ambrose socially visiting the Harper ranch.

In part the article stated: "Miles J. Ambrose, while U.S. commissioner of Customs, was the house guest last winter of a millionaire Texas rancher-banker who was then under investigation by Customs officials for smuggling.

"Six months later the Rancher Richmond C Harper was arrested with eight other men on charges of conspiring to smuggle 10,000 weapons into Mexico in exchange for 25 kilos of heroin."

The article further stated that undercover Agent Diosdado had testified that he had reported to the Mexico City U.S. Embassy on May 26 on BNDD Agent Arthur Sedillo's request to investigate a group of gun smugglers. "This group had approximately 10,000 assorted weapons, and they were trying to attempt to trade the weapons for 25 kilos of heroin.

"Agent Diosdado met with the suspects and placed his initial order for 3,500 to 4,500 M-1 rifles, 250 to 350 Thompson submachine guns, and 1,500 M-16 rifles, with 500 rounds of ammunition for each weapon.

"Harper then put Agent Diosdado in touch with Kessler, who invited him to visit him at a tool company in Newark where they manufactured the weapons.

"An additional million dollar transaction was made in exchange for explosives. Two other Customs agents flew to Shreveport to verify delivery and loading of explosives on a DC-4 as planned before Diosdado was to pay off Kessler in New Orleans.

"U.S. Customs agents Fernando Maldonado and Paul Provencio seized the plane and explosives. All the suspects, including Harper; Marion Hagler, a retired Immigration and Naturalization Service inspector; and Murray Kessler were arrested. Kessler has a record of six convictions in Federal and state courts on charges of interstate theft, transportation of stolen property, bookmaking, and conspiracy to possession of heroin. Federal authorities describe him as an associate of the Carlo Gambino organized-crime family."

Now here comes the kicker. It just so happened that U.S. Customs Director Miles Ambrose had previously partied at the Harper border ranch while he was the U.S. Customs national director, even though his subordinates had told him of Harper's reputation. As a result of Ambrose's social association with Harper, his selection as DEA administrator was compromised.

Without knowing Ambrose, but subsequently hearing that basically he was a good man, I felt sorry for him in his situation; however, he caused the replacement of Regional Director Arpaio with former U.S. Customs supervisor Bob Dean, who in coordination with Agent Bruce Van Matre kicked me out of contention for the Costa Rica DEA Attaché post. I felt that justice had been served.

Going back to my Mexico DEA tour of duty, I felt my career development was obstructed, but lo and behold, before the Costa Rica post was confirmed, Jerry Strickler at the DEA headquarters telephoned me and told me that as a result of a possible attempted assault on Bolivia DEA Attaché Marcelino Bedolla, he and his family had been immediately evacuated from La Paz, Bolivia. Jerry told me that if I wanted, he would recommend me to become Bolivia's U.S. Embassy DEA attaché.

I accepted that assignment, which included my promotion to GS-14. The irony of the transfer was that I got my GS-14 before Van Metre, since the Costa Rica DEA Attaché post had been delayed.

While all this was taking place and before I was transferred to Bolivia, Mexico City Regional Director Dean suffered a heart attack and died. His wife, whom I didn't know, came to the embassy, and after I had given her my condolences, she told me, "Actually I was looking for you and want to give you my husband's favorite gun holster. Bob knew you were a good man and didn't mean to harm you." She handed me a well-used leather snub-nosed pistol holster. I thanked her and within my heart forgave Regional Director Dean.

Robert Bob Eyman, however, another former U.S. Customs agent, became our Mexico City regional director. He and Agent Van Meter made no bones about being pissed with my promotion to Bolivia. It would not be the last I heard from those two.

The Costa Rican DEA office was finally confirmed, and Agent Van

Meter was assigned to that post as the attaché. Shortly after, however, he was kicked out for several improprieties, including purchasing a car from an informant.

Eventually Van Metre and Bob Eyman were transferred to DEA headquarters, and instead of Van Matre being punished for his misconduct in Costa Rica, he became my immediate supervisor, since he was assigned to work under Bob Eyman, who became in charge of the South American desk. Yes, those two guys would continue to harass me. I felt like two buckets of shit had been kicked and both landed on my head.

When I told my family that we were going to Bolivia, Mariana and the kids researched the place, learning as much as possible about the Andean country. They were all excited and looked forward to our new assignment. I kept counting my blessings for having such a loving and adventurous family.

We flew from Mexico City to Panama, where we had a week's layover. Panama DEA Agent in Charge Bruce Stock went on home leave with his family and insisted that we stay in his Canal Zone official residence.

We enjoyed the unexpected mini vacation and took advantage of the Canal Zone military post exchanges to stock up on items we would not have access to in Bolivia, which was considered a hardship post. We also enjoyed the beach, knowing Bolivia was landlocked.

When we arrived at the La Paz, Bolivia, International Airport, one of the highest airports in the world at 13,323 feet, we deplaned and experienced an altitude headache known in Bolivia as *sorochi*. Later we learned that the cure for sorochi was a tea made of coca leaves. The tea was even available in the U.S. Embassy cafeteria. For those who do not know, coca leaves alone are not illegal in Bolivia or Peru.

DEA Agent Gene Castillo and his wife, Joan, were standing by for us with both his official and personal Jeep station wagons, realizing that with five kids and several suitcases we would need both vehicles.

Gene and I traveled with the luggage, while Mariana and the kids went with Joan down to the La Paz residential area. Traveling on the dirt road was another indicator we had arrived in a third-world country.

Gene and Joan were also from New Mexico, and she had prepared us an excellent New Mexico-style supper that we enjoyed. While Joan briefed Mariana about the unique Bolivian lifestyle, including cooking tips at this high latitude, Gene briefed me on our mission. We spent the night at their place, since our residence would not be available until the following day.

The next morning, Gene and I reported to U.S. Ambassador Steadman and received a surprise. Ambassador Steadman, who was in his early sixties, was tall and slender and wore rimless glasses hanging on the tip of his nose. He pointed his bony finger at me in an admonishing manner and stated, "You are under house arrest, and under no circumstances are you to host government officials or meet, contact, or have any communication with anyone within our mission. Your agency has failed to follow protocol and request my concurrence in approving your assignment. Now get the hell out of here, and unless I hear from your headquarters immediately and explain why they didn't notify me of your assignment and wait for my approval, you may be on the next flight back to wherever the hell you came from."

I apologized to no avail, and as we walked out, I was shocked but impressed with Agent Castillo. He told the ambassador, "Mr. Ambassador, You are a son of a bitch!" The ambassador pointed in the direction of the door for us to get out of his office.

Agent Castillo sent an immediate cable to DEA headquarters, and we received a quick response apologizing to the ambassador, claiming that the oversight had been caused by the emergency evacuation of Agent Bedolla. The answer appeased the ambassador, permitting me to become operational.

After I was approved, my family and I went to our assigned two-story brick house secured by a ten-foot wall. The large yard included a swimming pool, but the majority of the time the water was freezing and rarely could be enjoyed.

DON'T EXPECT ANYTHING

We were surprised that there were no grocery stores or malls. The kids thought we had been kicked back a century in a time machine.

Mariana learned that once a week butchered cattle was flown into La Paz from the Beni, Bolivia, lowlands. The Bolivian *cholas* (women or girls), wearing derby hats and multilayered skirts, picked up slabs of meat at the airport and carried them over their shoulders down to selected residential sidewalk corners for sale to households. They also obtained vegetables and fruit cultivated in the Yungas lowlands. Truckloads of these products arrived in La Paz once a week and were also sold at designated street corners.

Because of the impoverished conditions, most of the diplomatic mission families were encouraged to hire the local cholas as maids to assist in multi-household duties. Besides having two maids, we had Don Gregorio, an elderly man who cut the lawn with a folded metal lid of a can. We tried to make him use a push lawn mower, but he refused to use it. He would get on his knees and trim the grass with his folded can top as he chewed coca leaves.

The Bolivian National Enforcement Unit (DNSP) director was an old retired military officer named Colonel Luis Carrasco. He was somewhat cordial but had little if any knowledge regarding drug enforcement activities. He failed to get involved in any operational activities.

His graciousness was mostly motivated by our financial assistance. For example the vehicle we purchased for DNSP was used by the director for his personal use. On all bilateral operations, we had to provide the transportation, per diem, and other related expenses.

Bolivia and neighboring Peru were the two legal coca cultivation countries in the world, and as such were the most prominent illegal manufacturers of cocaine. Just to understand the increase in illicit cocaine base production in Bolivia, when I arrived at this post, crude coca-base was processed in fifty-gallon steel barrels. The coca leaves were mixed with kerosene to extract the primary cocaine alkaloids. When these alkaloids were obtained, the kerosene from the barrels was drained by removing the barrel's bottom plug. The alkaloids are then mixed with other chemicals to produce the final illegal product, cocaine hydrochloride.

Within a few months, the primary raw cocaine producers replaced the fifty-gallon barrels with trenches two yards by four yards wide and one yard deep. Plastic sheets were placed in the trenches and kerosene was poured over much more massive amounts of coca leaves.

Producers used sharp wooden spikes to puncture the plastic bottom to drain the kerosene, and then the alkaloids were processed. Seeing those and other drug-trafficking developments, I kept asking DEA headquarters for additional agents, since Agent Castillo and I were constantly on the road. Even Ambassador Steadman concurred with my demands, to no avail. Keep in mind that the DEA headquarters supervisors of Latin American affairs were Eyman and Van Matre.

On February 19, 1975. our sixth child, Pablo, was born at Albuquerque, New Mexico, and that day too was one of my happiest days. I joined them after testifying in Miami, and we returned together to Bolivia.

The Caracas Regional Office recognized our problem, but unfortunately DEA Headquarters failed to respond. Finally, after I did much bitching, Agent Larry Lyons was added to our office, but we still needed additional agents.

David Arroyo, the U.S. Embassy Agency for International Development (U.S. AID) representative and retired Los Angeles Police Department detective assisted with other Bolivian police agencies, including Customs. We worked together to complement both our missions.

Ambassador Stedman backed me up in my diplomatic effort to solicit the attorney generals and narcotics enforcement directors in countries surrounding Bolivia to attend a conference in Bolivia.

David Arroyo and I bypassed the DNSP director and met with Colonel Juan Pereda Asbun, the Bolivian minister of the interior, who accepted my recommendation to invite the appropriate officials from the surrounding countries. The minister recommended that we

DON'T EXPECT ANYTHING

conduct the conference at Cochabamba, Bolivia, so that our guests would not have problems with the high La Paz altitude.

Before we had the conference, I talked the Minister into having Bolivian President Banzer sign the International Narcotic Enforcement Treaty known as the United Nations Single Convention of 1961; which in part, binds all the members to cooperate in international drug enforcement efforts. Colonel Pereda Asbun quickly obtained presidential approval, and the convention was signed.

After this was done, the Bolivian government sent out formal invitations to its neighboring countries' officials, including those in Peru, Chile, Brazil, Argentina, and Paraguay, and all these countries agreed to participate.

The conference was conducted in July 1975 at the Cochabamba Hotel, which facilitated us with two large meeting rooms plus individual hotel rooms for our guests.

After the opening ceremony welcoming speech by Minister Pereda Asbun, he and all the attorney generals went to one conference room. David and I accompanied the national police and narcotics enforcement directors to the second conference room. We assured the minister of the Interior that we would maintain a low profile, making it appear that the convention was a Bolivian government initiative.

The first meeting almost ended in a street fight. I hoped we had not created a mini war. Each representative blamed the others for the increased cocaine trafficking, and each kept bragging about its country's accomplishments.

I kept looking at Dave Arroyo, letting him know that we had to do something before the thing got entirely out of control. David, like a wise old bull, winked his eye and raised his forefinger to his nose, telling me to calm down. He stood up and made the timeout signal with his hands, interrupted the bickering, and said:

"Gentlemen, at this point we are going to have a ten-minute break to go to the restroom or whatever."

When they took the break, David told me to follow him to his room. We picked up two boxes containing scotch, tequila, pisco sour, and several mixes. We also stopped at the café and obtained a tub of ice cubes and two trays of glasses.

When the group returned, David and I invited them all to fix a drink of their choice and continue with the conference.

In no time the participants contributed positive suggestions for better international cooperation. Mean hand waving was replaced with handshakes and macho hugs.

During the next three days, we had several of our meetings and breaks outside and enjoyed the Cochabamba eternal spring weather. We played the Bolivian Sapo (Toad) game. Reportedly based on an Incan legend, the game involves throwing lead coins into a metal toad's open mouth from a distance of two meters. One of the rules of the game was that the participant had to hold a cocktail drink on the hand not being used to toss the metal coins, a rule we didn't have a hard time enforcing. We noticed that besides having a positive conference, several long-lasting friendships developed among the participants.

At the end of the conference, Bolivian President Banzer and the minister of the interior participated in the closing ceremony. As a result of this meeting, follow-up conferences were conducted in the other participating countries.

Immediately after the conference, DNSP started getting actionable intelligence reports from other conference members, but most importantly, the minister of the interior and President Banzer realized that their DNSP national director had to be replaced with a better qualified director.

Colonel Aparicio Coca, who was the complete opposite of his predecessor, became the new DNSP national director. Colonel Aparicio was an ex-Catholic seminarian and a God-fearing, honest, and super intelligent man. He immediately made the needed changes in management and operational activities. Under his command the agency became most effective.

One of his first administrative changes was to appoint Colonel

Rodolfo Tapia as his deputy director. Colonel Tapia spoke fluent English, which was an added positive thing in the sense that he participated in the interrogation of American and other English-speaking international suspects. The director also appointed Dr. Noya to head the drug rehabilitation section.

Another major positive accomplishment made by the new DNSP administrator was establishing a closer working relationship with Bolivian Customs officials at the La Paz International Airport.

We taught the Customs officials how to profile potential drug trafficking suspects. Each time a possible suspect arrived at the airport, DNSP and our office were notified so that we could initiate surveillance on the suspects.

Shortly afterward, a young American couple arrived at the La Paz International Airport. They met the drug courier profile, and Bolivian Customs notified DNSP and our office that the suspects would be staying at the La Paz Holiday Inn Hotel.

We rented a room next to the American suspects, and on the following day, Bolivian suspect Ramon arrived at their hotel room and delivered three kilograms of cocaine to them.

The three were arrested, and immediately we separated the Americans from the Bolivian suspect. Upon interrogating the American suspects, we learned that a Los Angeles, California, trafficker had talked them into coming to La Paz and picking up the three kilograms of cocaine. They were instructed on how to hide the cocaine in secret compartments of a suitcase.

The American suspects also told us that Ramon was to accompany them back to the United States and that he would be the one delivering the cocaine to the Los Angeles suspect.

The American suspects, whom we will refer to as Jack and Jill, agreed to cooperate with us, but Ramon refused and was imprisoned.

I telephoned the Los Angeles, California, DEA office and said that we had flipped the American suspects and they had agreed to play the role that I was their Bolivian associate. I would be accompanying the suspects and make a controlled delivery of the three kilograms of cocaine to the L.A. trafficker.

The L.A. DEA office agreed to the plan. On January 31, 1976, Jack and Jill, as well as Bolivian DNSP Agents Kalifa and Ray accompanied me to Los Angeles, California.

We met with the L.A. DEA agents at the downtown Holiday Inn, where we rented three rooms, one for Jack and Jill, one for the Bolivian agents, and one for me. My room was in the middle of the other two with connecting doors.

Since we arrived late at night, we agreed that we would not telephone the suspect until the following day. Late that night I heard my Bolivian buddies laughing and shouting. I wondered what the hell they were doing and entered their room. They had moved one of their beds near the window, which they had opened. They both sat on the bed and were looking at the traffic on the freeway. They explained to me that they had never seen so many cars at the same time.

On the following day at about 6:00 p.m., we had Jack and Jill telephone the suspect and tell him to go directly to my room, letting him know that I spoke English. He came and knocked on my room door.

I opened the door, and after exchanging greetings, I showed him the opened suitcase, exposing the cocaine. He took out his bulky wallet and started counting the money. The local agents monitored my room, and upon hearing us terminate the transaction, they burst into the room, arrested the suspect, and seized the money and the cocaine.

After receiving an outstanding evaluation rating by Caracas regional management that recommended my promotion to a regional management position, Van Matre and Robert J. Eyman downgraded my evaluation.

I could not take this shit anymore and raised hell with Van Matre on a telephone call. I was ordered to proceed to DEA headquarters on the next available flight.

At DEA headquarters I got my ass chewed out by Eyman and Van Matre and was threatened to be fired unless I apologized to Van Matre.

I ate crow and did apologize, even though I was not sincere. I was not going to compromise my career because of those two.

Eyman later traveled to Bolivia after Ambassador Steadman prohibited his visit, telling DEA headquarters that I was too busy to be interrupted by him. Eyman disregarded the ambassador's orders and traveled to La Paz, Bolivia, anyway. Upon learning this, Ambassador Steadman prohibited Eyman from coming to the embassy. I had to meet him at a street corner, like meeting with a snitch. He chewed my ass out for not being able to control the ambassador. I took him to the airport, and while he continued chewing me out, I just smiled, further pissing him off.

The ambassador who had originally placed me under house arrest requested DEA headquarters to extend my two-year hardship post an additional year, which was granted.

It is interesting to note that sometime after I was transferred out of Bolivia, *DEA World* magazine reported that the La Paz Country DEA office not only increased it number of personnel, but it also added sub-offices in other Bolivian sites. It became the second largest foreign post.

CHAPTER 25

MY FAMILY MEMBERS and I had mixed feelings when we left Bolivia, in the sense that our exposure to the hardship post had given us the opportunity to better appreciate what we had when compared to many in that impoverished country. We had made many friends within the mission and among Bolivian nationals. We would miss them all. My daughters Athena and Rita graduated from high school with honors and were looking forward to attending college at the Panama Canal Zone. Andrew and Gino were excited, knowing that they would be playing American football in high school. Emiliano and Pablo would continue being spoiled at home.

When we arrived in Panama, we were expecting to reside on the Canal Zone like all DEA predecessors, but as a result of the ongoing negotiations to return the U.S. Canal Zone to the Panamanian government, we would have to reside within the Republic of Panama like the rest of the American diplomatic personnel.

We were a bit upset until we saw our Panamanian residence. The beautiful white five-bedroom mansion-like home rested on top of a well-manicured grass hill surrounded by coconut palm trees. The view from the house veranda included old Colonial Panama ruins and the seacoast.

When we finally settled in, a young boy carrying a bucket rang our doorbell. He was selling lobsters for a dollar each. We purchased all he had and became his regular customer.

The one thing that didn't change workwise was that the Panama DEA office also had only one agent besides the supervisor position. When I arrived, Agent Sheldon E. Reyher had expected to be named the new SAIC and was not pleased to see me come aboard.

I sympathized with Sheldon and told him that we were both in the same boat in the sense that I had expected to be promoted to a higher management position. I told him we would have to do the best we could for our personal and professional tranquility.

During my first meeting with the ambassador and his staff I was informed that the mission's number-one priority was the diplomatic processing of the U.S. Canal Zone to the Panamanian Republic.

I was instructed to intensify our bilateral narcotics enforcement efforts because of the ongoing political unrest. When I asked for further clarification, I was informed that the Chief of Panamanian Government Omar Torrijos brother had been implicated in illicit drug trafficking and that the anti-treaty U.S. politicians kept bringing up that issue.

I was told that my direct contact with the Panamanian government would be National Director of Intelligence Lieutenant Colonel Manuel Noriega. I was instructed to meet him as soon as possible and to keep the mission posted on our activities.

I drove to Sergeant Major Jorge Latinez's office in one of two military complexes that were separated by a regular city street in an impoverished Panamanian housing zone.

Latinez was a slender man in his mid-forties with deep-set eyes and a receding hairline. He was the intermediate contact to Colonel Noriega.

When I entered his office, he stood at attention, giving me a sharp military salute and immediately burst out laughing, welcoming me aboard in a friendly fashion.

After shaking hands and exchanging introductions, Latinez quickly added, "We were looking forward to your arrival, and hopefully we will develop a good working relationship."

"I can assure you, Sergeant that those are my intentions."

He said, "My friends, which I will include you as of this moment, call me Lino, so please, let's knock off formalities."

We walked across the street to the headquarters' command post where a female military lieutenant escorted us into Colonel Noriega's office.

Lieutenant Colonel Noriega was a man in his early forties and about five feet six inches tall. He welcomed me in a friendly manner and asked that we join him in his conference room.

After introductions, he ordered his receptionist to bring us iced tea. Lieutenant Colonel Noriega told me in so many words the same thing the U.S. Mission had empathized that his top priority was recuperating the Canal Zone through our combined diplomatic efforts.

Without mentioning Head of State Omar's brother's drug-trafficking allegation, Noriega said that it was important that we intensify our bilateral drug enforcement efforts and that his door would always be open to me around the clock.

He instructed Lino to introduce me to the Panamanian Customs director as well as the national chief of police, and he assured me that those organizations would support our combined enforcement efforts. Even though the meeting lasted only about fifteen minutes, I felt it had gone well.

Lino complied with Colonel Noriega's instructions and immediately telephoned these other officials followed by our visiting them. I also got a positive reaction regarding their willingness to cooperate.

Lino and I met with Panamanian Customs Supervisor Octavio Rodriguez and talked about profiling potential transshipment suspects, as well as aircraft traveling to cocaine source countries and back to the United States through Panama.

To further implement this plan, Customs officials were instructed to immediately telephone Lino and me with the identification of any suspect pilots and passengers as well as the aircraft N-number. Our office would, in turn, pass that information to the FAA officials at the Canal Zone and to concerned domestic DEA offices, so the suspects and aircraft could be further identified and placed on a lookout list. Once we established that the suspect aircrafts and people met the profile of a trafficker, they would be intercepted upon their return. Lino also passed this information on to other airports within the Republic of Panama.

Agent Reyher then took me to the Canal Zone, where we met the U.S. attorney, the Canal Zone Customs officials, and military law enforcement officials as well as the Federal Aviation Administration (FAA) supervisor.

A couple of days later, Lino telephoned me to say that the police had arrested a major Colombian National trafficker, Luis Bernardo Londono-Quintero. Unfortunately our domestic offices had not yet indicted him, so he couldn't be extradited to the United States. When he was arrested, he had no illicit drugs in his possession.

Lino told me, "I don't give a shit whether you guys have enough evidence on him or not. We all know he is a major trafficker. He even offered me a bribe to cut him loose."

Upon learning of this arrest, Lieutenant Colonel Manuel Noriega ordered that Lino and I report immediately to his office. When we got there, he chewed our asses out because incidents of arresting people without evidence were exactly what the anti-Canal Zone-exchange politicians wanted to hear. They would claim that the government was violating human rights.

He yelled at us, "What the hell are you going to do with this case?"

I told Noriega, "Colonel, Londono offered Lino a bribe to be released and that he had money in a local Colombian bank. Why don't you let Lino accept the bribe and then charge Londono with attempting to bribe a public official?"

Noriega silently stared at me with his itty-bitty eyes, and all of a sudden burst out laughing and instructed us, "Go the hell out there right now and do that. We can't have anyone in jail without being charged."

When Lino and I were on our way to get the bribe from Londono, he told me, "You know, Art, Noriega really likes you, and I can tell by the way he chewed both our asses out. He didn't give a shit about diplomacy and treated you like one of us."

Lino borrowed a wig from his wife to wear when he took Londono to the Colombian bank. He and one of his men escorted the suspect to the Colombian bank while I followed a few steps behind. Londono withdrew $50,000 and handed the money to Lino, who in turn placed him under arrest for attempting to bribe a public official.

Lino later told me that Noriega was placing that seized money in the narcotics enforcement budget.

On April 26, 1979, Lino telephoned me and said that his people in David, Panama, a small village on the border with Costa Rica, had called him to say that a small aircraft with an American serial number N227F had crash-landed near their airstrip. Two American suspects had been arrested after several kilograms of cocaine were found in the crashed plane.

I had a U.S. consular officer accompany Lino and me to David, Panama, so he could verify that the defendants' rights were not violated. Upon our arrival, we inspected the crashed aircraft, and with the assistance of the local authorities, removed several suitcases containing a cocaine shipment that was subsequently estimated to be worth two million dollars in the U.S. market. (6)

The two Americans were identified as Jorge Luis Valdes of Miami, Florida, and Harold Rosenthal of Atlanta, Georgia. After we interviewed them and they failed to admit their involvement, they were extradited to the United States where they were prosecuted and imprisoned.

Apparently suspect Jorge Luis Valdez, after his imprisonment,

　　　　　　　　　　　DON'T EXPECT ANYTHING

repented and became a religious preacher, according to his published book.

The more I worked with Lino, the more he impressed me. He spoke fluent English and three other languages. He was super intelligent and was considered one of very few Noriega's confidants.

One day he telephoned me to say to meet him at the Panamanian Customs office at the international airport because the Customs supervisor had a potential cooperating individual for me. At the Customs office I met Supervisor Gonzales and Lino and a Panamanian pilot named Floyd Carlton. He had been detained for falsifying his pilot credentials as well as possible Peruvian violations. When he was interviewed he claimed to have knowledge about international drug trafficking, so the Customs officials turned him over to me to be documented as a cooperating individual

A couple of weeks later Carlton phoned me to say to come to the airport because he wanted to show me something of interest. I met him at the international airport, and from there we walked to a private hangar where seven dead Cuban bodies were laid out on a table. He told me that they were killed in the Sandinista war going on in Honduras and were being returned to Cuba. Carlton told me, "Colonel Noriega instructed me to pass this information to you so that you could report it to your government."

Even though I found it strange that Colonel Noriega was in contact with Carlton, I did report the information to our mission.

During my last days at that post, Lino telephoned me and told me that Noriega wanted to give me a small yacht as a farewell gift for my service to their country and that a Panamanian ship would deliver it to me near Houston, Texas. I told him to thank Noriega for his generosity, but we were prohibited from receiving any expensive gifts.

When we moved out of our house to the Holiday Inn so that our furniture could be packed and shipped to the United States, Lieutenant Colonel Noriega, accompanied by Lino, came to the hotel to bid me farewell. He handed me a wrapped gift, and I cautioned him it could not be an expensive item. He told me, "I know, I know. Lino told me." After exchanging hugs and saying good-bye, they departed.

I opened the wrapped gift hoping it was something like a wristwatch or camera. It was a damn glass ashtray with the emblem of the Panamanian flag embedded on the base. He reduced the gift price range from a yacht to an ashtray.

I received an outstanding ambassador's evaluation and several "atta boys" from Manuel Noriega, including a farewell official memorandum that states in translation:

"Dear Mr. Regional Director Arturo Sedillo:

"Upon terminating your mission in the Republic of Panama, it is my obligation to recognize the magnificent and coordinated professional work that you carried out in our geographical area.

"Your labor was far beyond that of a functionary administrator, and you practically constituted yourself into a National Panamanian Soldier at war against the enemies of youth's health, which are the illicit drug traffickers.

"In you we always found, at any given hour, the man ready to carry out the missions and responsibilities.

"With you we were able to have the best results in our fight against the criminals involved in the dirty business of drug trafficking.

"With you we were able to put the Republic of Panama in the first place of integrity and champions against this fight.

"In our relations with you, there was good faith, professional capacity, material disinterest, honesty, and the knowledge that Panama was and is a permanent ally of the United States in this fight.

"We bid you farewell because we know that wherever you may be, there will be a Panamanian and a soldier in the fight against the criminals that corrupt, causing sickness and killing humanity with drug trafficking.

"Sincerely Yours, Lieutenant Colonel Manuel A. Noriega"

The U.S. Embassy deputy chief of mission's evaluation of my performance stated in part:

DON'T EXPECT ANYTHING

"Mr. Sedillo has done a superb job in advancing United States' interests in Panama over the past two years. During this time he has contributed significantly to a complete turnaround of the Panamanian Government concerning cooperation with the U.S. in the drug interdiction program. In the process, Mr. Sedillo has developed high-level law enforcement and intelligence relationships and contacts that have been useful to the Embassy in areas outside the narcotics field.

"Arrests of traffickers and narcotics seizures have broken all previous records during the past year—a record of which Mr. Sedillo is justly proud. Equally important, however, is his encouragement of Panama's participation in the development of international conspiracy cases. This has caused a number of expulsions of U.S. citizens to the USA where they have testified against major traffickers who hired them as couriers, thus serving the cause of greater justice. It has also resulted in the identification and immobilization of major sources of supply in South America."

Receiving these "Atta-boys" and learning that my next assignment would be as the agent in charge of the Laredo, Texas, DEA resident office further cheered me up, knowing that the Laredo office supervisor's rank was a GS-15 position.

Mariana and the kids were even more excited than I was, learning that Athena and Rita would attend the University of Texas in Austin, Texas. Andrew and Gino would be playing football at Laredo High School, while Emiliano and Paul would be attending the elementary school.

My last official duty in the Panama U.S. Embassy was to send a cable to DEA headquarters with copies to the Laredo, Texas, DEA Office that I would be arriving at the Laredo Airport on the evening of July 24, 1979, and for the Laredo DEA office to please make hotel reservations for two connecting rooms. I would also need assistance transporting my family and twelve suitcases.

CHAPTER 25

CHAPTER 26

AFTER TEN YEARS of my being on foreign assignments, the family was overjoyed to return to the United States. When we landed at the Laredo, Texas, airport and set foot at the tarmac, seven-year-old Emiliano kneeled and kissed it. He proclaimed, "Thank God we are back in the United States."

The rest of us were amazed by his youthful patriotism. His brothers teased him, reminding him that he was born in Mexico City. "But as a U.S. citizen," I added.

After waiting for more than an hour for DEA assistance, I remembered that our domestic offices were indifferent to family matters. DEA: Don't Expect Anything.

I started to contact a taxi cab, when two DEA agents arrived. They apologized for being late, telling me that they had come on their own because Supervisor Cochran had failed to notify anyone of our arrival and requested assistance. Grace Shoup, the office secretary, had discreetly tipped off those agents about our arrival after Cochran had destroyed the cable I had sent.

I appreciated the risk those guys took in assisting us. They came in their own cars so that Cochran could not bitch if he learned that they had helped us.

When I reported to the office the following day, Supervisor Cochran was less than pleasant. He barely acknowledged me, telling me that I would not be able to move into his office until he departed. If his intentions were to piss me off, I told him, "Hell, I would not want to be in the office until you and all your shit are out of it." He didn't respond, and the following day he departed to DEA headquarters

At the same time of Cochran's transfer, I learned that the Laredo DEA office supervisor position had been downgraded from a GS-15 to a GS-14 grade; therefore, my promotion was again stalled. Since I had received outstanding evaluations from regional DEA management, the U.S. ambassadors, and host government officials, I could have challenged headquarters but knew that it would be a waste of time. Nonetheless, I could not help thinking that my continually being deprived of a promotion was because of the previously identified agents and the fact that I had indirectly contributed to causing former U.S. Customs Commissioner Miles Ambrose from becoming the first DEA administrator. That atmosphere gave birth to the title of this book, *DEA: Don't Expect Anything.*

Mariana got a job at Doctor's Hospital as the nurses' secretary and within a short time was promoted to personnel director. The job not only demonstrated Mariana's outstanding abilities but it also opened the door for both our teenage sons, Andrew and Gino, to get a part-time job in the hospital. As a result of this exposure, they were motivated to pursue the medical profession, and both become eminent doctors.

One of the first things I did when the office was turned over to my command was to telephone my friend and former Mexico City DEA supervisor Jack Compton. He had transferred to U.S. Customs in Laredo, Texas, where he became the Customs Patrol Unit supervisor.

Jack told me that of a tradition within the local law enforcement agencies to welcome newcomers by celebrating at a formal party. He told me to please wear a suit and tie and that the event was a strictly guy thing, so no wives were invited. He said, "I will pick you up this Friday at 5:00 p.m., so be sure to be standing by for me."

I agreed.

That Friday afternoon after picking me up, Jack drove to the outskirts of the city where we got off the highway to a dirt road and onto a barren hillside.

We arrived where a makeshift barbecue pit was cooking meat, surrounded by fifteen lawmen all dressed in Levis and casual shirts and drinking beer. They all burst out laughing, seeing me all dressed, letting me know that it was a traditional initiation for all newcomers.

I must admit that it was an excellent way to meet several law enforcement representatives, making it easier for coordination later on in multilateral enforcement operations.

Since the Laredo DEA office had been downgraded, my immediate supervisor was McAllen, Texas, DEA District Supervisor Ken Miley, who approved that I form a mini multi-agency task force including U.S. Customs representatives and Laredo Police Department detectives. During the initiation, we didn't include a Webb County sheriff's representative, because information indicated that its narcotics supervisor was corrupt.

Several Laredo police detectives, including Raul Perez, Candelario Viera, Frank Romanilli, and Joe Hernandez were assigned to our office task force. My buddy Jack Compton also appointed U.S Customs Agent Michael Waggoner and Agent Bill Pullen to the unit.

Sometime after, DEA Agent Hector Berrelles, stationed on the West Coast, had been working in an undercover capacity and had penetrated an organization that included Laredo, Texas, Webb County Sheriff's Head of Narcotics Division Supervisor Jose Luis Muñoz. West Coast-assigned Agent Berrelles coordinated with our office to purchase a kilogram of heroin from Muñoz.

On the afternoon of the night that the deal was supposed to go down, Muñoz telephoned me and told me, "Art, an informant is expected to give me some information about a drug shipment coming from Mexico through here and on to Dallas, Texas. Please be standing by for my telephone call at your house, and I will call you if the information is positive."

I told him okay. Needless to say, I was out that evening with our troops when Muñoz sold the kilogram of heroin to our undercover DEA agent.

When we busted his ass, I told him, "Sorry, Muñoz, that I was not able to stay home waiting for your telephone call, because I knew you were the scumbag trafficker in question."

He just bowed his head, speechless, as officials incarcerated his ass on charges of selling heroin to an undercover DEA agent.

After his arrest, I met with Sheriff Mario Santos and assured him that we knew he wasn't aware of Muñoz's involvement in drug traffic.

He was most apologetic and thanked me for my comments. He told me that he was aware of our multi-agency task force and he would like to assign an honorable member of the Webb County sheriff's office to join our task force. He said, "Because of the damn embarrassment Muñoz has brought to our agency, I have disbanded the Narcotics Unit. If you agree with my proposition, I want you and your men to select the deputy you want to be assigned to your task force."

That same day we had an office meeting, and all agreed on selecting Webb County Sheriff Deputy J. J. Perez, whom they identified as a loyal, honest, and hardworking deputy.

When I met with Sheriff Mario Santos and told him who we had selected, he broke into a big smile and told me, "I want you to lift my desk office calendar and see the name I hoped you would select."

I did as instructed, and the piece of paper had Deputy Sheriff J. J. Perez's name on it. Not only was Agent J. J. Perez an excellent detective, but he also quickly proved his professional abilities. In coordination with DEA Agent Max Pooly, J. J. Perez worked undercover meeting a major Colombian drug trafficker who, after several international telephone calls, traveled to Laredo, Texas, and delivered five kilograms of cocaine to J. J. Perez.

As a result of this investigation and several others, U.S. Customs hired J. J. Perez as a regular U.S. Customs agent, which he well deserved.

In Laredo, Texas, for the next two years, our task force and office agents were always busy. Besides initiating our own cases, the U.S. Border Patrol regularly called us to travel wherever it needed us to retrieve drugs seized from illegal aliens the patrol had busted within our extended area of responsibility.

While I was stationed in Laredo, my good friend Panamanian Sergeant Major Jorge "Lino" Latinez wrote me a letter telling me that General Noriega had gone wrong, getting involved in taking bribes from major drug traffickers.

Noriega learned that Lino had exposed him as a trafficker and sent him to Cuba, where the doctors conducted a lobotomy, leaving him like a vegetable. A friend told me that he had seen Lino selling pencils and umbrellas on a Panama City street corner and that he was almost totally incoherent.

After Noriega was arrested and extradited to the United States and prosecuted in the Miami, Florida, Federal Court, two other former DEA Panama supervisors and I were subpoenaed by the defense to testify in favor of Noriega. I testified that we had a good working relationship but that I was careful not to share sensitive information with him that was not developed bilaterally. I attempted to tell the court what he had done to Lino, sending him to Cuba to get a lobotomy, but the defense objected.

During this trial I learned that the Miami DEA office's main witness against Noriega was informant Floyd Carlton, whom I had originally documented as our cooperating individual (CI) in Panama.

Noriega's book, *The Memoirs of Manuel Noriega, America's Prisoner,* gave Floyd Carlton a different spin. He said, "My principal accuser at the drug trial was Floyd Carlton Caceres, a Panamanian pilot, who testified that he had paid me hush money so that he could ship loads of cocaine from Colombia to Panama and onward to the United States in the early 1980s. I believe him when he says that he is transporting drugs. But I had nothing to do with it.

"I had been told by the Drug Enforcement Administration and by the CIA that Carlton, who had delivered guns for the CIA to pro-American Nicaraguan rebels, was an undercover drug agent who should be left alone. The word came when our agents had arrested Carlton on an international warrant issued by the Peruvian Investigative Police. 'Release him to our custody,' DEA Station Chief Arthur Sedillo told Latinez (Lino), his Panamanian liaison.

"'Carlton works for us; we're taking care of him,' Sedillo said. 'Let him go about his business; we will monitor his operations.'

"So, instead of being subjected to a pending Panamanian indictment and instead of being extradited to the jurisdiction of Peruvian authorities as we had intended, Carlton was released to Sedillo's custody without any documentation whatsoever. The United States never gives documentation to lowly countries like Panama. All they do is ask you for a favor—and you go along with it or reject it, but you never learn the details, nor the results, nor what deals have been made."

Noriega was not only found guilty and imprisoned, but subsequently continued doing time in a Panamanian prison as well.

CHAPTER 27

IN JULY 1984, Mexico City DEA Regional Director Edward Heath visited Mariana and me, and we had him over for dinner. He asked me to become his agent in charge of the Monterrey, Mexico, resident office.

I had always had the highest admiration and respect for Director Heath. I knew him from our Miami, Florida, Task Force Operation Eagle days where we, the "dirty dozen" undercover agents team, assisted in immobilizing major Cuban American drug trafficking organizations.

After that operation, Agent Heath had been shot by a trafficker. He survived his facial wound; however, his brother, DEA Agent Richard Heath, who was the agent in charge of the Quito, Ecuador, U.S. Embassy DEA office was shot while working in an undercover capacity and subsequently died as a result of that assault.

Since higher management had no intention of promoting me to a GS-15 position, I figured returning to a foreign assignment would be to my family's economic advantage. Besides that, it would be my last tour of duty before I retired. I accepted Regional Director Heath's offer.

The transfer from Laredo, Texas, to Monterey, Mexico, on July 8, 1984, was the shortest transfer I made in distance, 150 miles, which we drove in three hours.

That foreign assignment was my first to a U.S. Consulate instead of a U.S. Embassy. The U.S. consulate general was the chief honcho at the Consulate, and he reported to the Mexico City U.S. ambassador within the Department of State chain of command.

On my reporting date, July 8, 1984, Consulate General Heflin had a staff meeting to introduce me to the rest of the mission officers. The consulate general and I became good friends, and he was most supportive of my recommended improvements to our mini-DEA office.

Agents assigned to the Monterey office included Agents Jimmy Garza, a former U.S. Marine captain; Jose Aguilar, a former teacher; Frank Fernandez, a young New Yorker; and Eddy Martinez. Agent Aguilar humorously told me that he became a narcotics agent because teaching had become too dangerous.

Monterrey was a transshipment point for illicit narcotics from Mexico to the United States; however, besides Monterrey, Nuevo Leon, our office was also responsible for the surrounding states of Durango, Coahuila, and Tamaulipas.

Besides working within my area of responsibility, I became the only field supervisor to get involved in Operation Vanguard. The operation, initiated by Mexico City Regional Director Edward Heath, involved agents participating with MFJP agents verifying the destruction of opium and marijuana plantations within the Republic of Mexico.

The operation became unpopular with some agents, and they bitched that the risk of flying in helicopters and fixed-wing aircraft identifying and verifying the destruction of illicit cultivation was too dangerous and beyond their job description.

Some MFJP pilots and Mexican agents were killed during those field operations while spraying illicit cultivation. On several occasions when I flew with them, we found that the illicit drug cultivators tied metal cables across the opium fields between mountainsides so that fumigating MFJP helicopters would crash. On other occasions, I observed and participated in shootouts between MFJP agents in helicopters and illicit cultivators. My feeling was that it was the real drug war.

On December 31, 1988, I retired from the DEA after twenty-four years of federal service. It included my four years in the U.S. Marines and twenty years in the DEA and its predecessor agencies. Athena and Rita graduated from the University of Texas in Austin, Texas. Andrew and Gino remained in Monterrey, Mexico, attending the prestigious University of Monterrey Medical University. After obtaining their doctorate medical degrees, they continued doing their residency at the University of Texas Medical School in Corpus Christi, Texas. Andrew became a psychiatrist and Gino became a cardiologist. Emiliano joined the U.S. Marines and worked in radio recon, where he received several combat ribbons and the rank of sergeant. After his tour of duty, he became a Naval Criminal Investigative Service agent and later on, a U.S. Homeland Security agent. Pablo continued his education at the University of Texas. Two days after I retired from DEA, Mariana and I moved to Mexico City, where I was hired by the U.S. Embassy Department of State Narcotics Affairs Unit for five years, where I replaced all previous DEA agents conducting Operation Vanguard illicit crop verification activities. Mariana was employed by the U.S. Embassy as a consular visa officer and later as the U.S. Embassy commissary manager.

During that time frame, I also conducted the murder investigation of six Jesuit priests in El Salvador, and my findings implicated Salvadorian military officers, as reported in *The Washington Post* that in part stated:

"One U.S. official who investigated the Jesuit murders and who was not deaf, dumb, and blind was Arthur Sedillo, the veteran DEA undercover agent who worked as a consultant to the State Department. During the course of his independent inquiry on behalf of the U.S. Embassy, Sedillo repeatedly raised the possibility with his colleagues that the Jesuit murders were the result of a conspiracy that extended beyond the lower-ranking soldiers that had been charged in the case. Sedillo's investigatory on the murders raised questions about Captain

DON'T EXPECT ANYTHING

Herrera—the CIA officer's companion to the site of the killings.

"One key to the analysis of Sedillo's of the crime was the November 13 search of the Jesuit residence. Sedillo wrote that he 'firmly believed' this was evidence linking the search to the murders on November 16. One fact that supported this hypothesis, Sedillo said, was the presence of the DNI officer, Lieutenant Hector Cuenca Ocampo, on the search mission. He recommended that the U.S. Mission find out the name of Cuenca Ocampo's commanding officer at DNI.

"'You find out who this guy was reporting to, and it would be the link to higher military echelon where they were trying to deny culpability,' Sedillo said.

"The CIA was the proper agency to respond to inquiries about the NNI. Sedillo's memo was disseminated to the agency representative on the task force in March 1990, according to one official familiar with the work. Did the CIA respond to Sedillo's question?

"An agency spokesman said he did not know the answer to that question, that the identity of the DNI officer in question was not a secret and that the name was easily obtainable by many of the agencies represented on the U.S. Embassy task force.

"The name was Captain Carlos Herrera. Months later, Cuenca Herrera told the Salvadorian investigators that he had acted on the orders of Captain Herrera. The head of the DNI said the same thing. Herrera, according to a statement he later gave to investigators, was acting director of operations of DNI at the time. Taken together, these statements indicate that Herrera had authorized intelligence gathering of the Jesuits two days before the killings. That raised the possibility of DNI involvement in an assassination conspiracy, a line of inquiry that was not vigorously pursued.

"The full truth about the U.S. government's investigation of the Jesuit murders may not be known until President Clinton's declassification directive is carried out. The CIA, in its initial effort to comply with the order, searched all of its data bases and found thousands of references to the Jesuit murders alone, a veritable top-secret encyclopedia in which may lie answers to the lingering mysteries of one of the most notorious political murders of recent years."

Several of the Salvadorian military officers, up to Colonel Guillermo Alfredo Benavides Moreno, director of the Military Academy, were prosecuted for those murders.

Back in Mexico City, after learning that an attorney general special unit was conducting surveillance on me for conducting unilateral illicit drug cultivation verification flights with another U.S. agency pilot, I knew that it was time to go home.

I was a contract worker for another U.S. agency for an additional five years. After that, my wife and I worked on several wire taps for the DEA, FBI, and U.S. Customs throughout the United States. I later became a Texas private investigator, municipal judge, and active member of our Catholic church Knights of Columbus, being thankful to God, my wife, and my family for a wonderful life.

CONCLUSION

IN THE LATE 1980s, famous news reporter Harry Reasoner asked the Mexican attorney general, "How can you stop the flow of illicit drugs from your country into the United States?"

The attorney general answered, "When your citizens stop the demand, because it is a problem of supply and demand."

After I worked forty years in law enforcement, from local to national and international levels, people constantly ask my opinion regarding the cause of drug abuse. I answer them that there may be a bit of truth to the theory of supply and demand, but I think the problem is because of the lack of love and discipline in families.

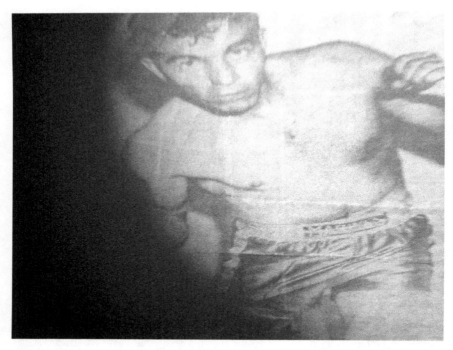

(1) Las Vegas, Nevada, Tri-state Golden Glove Championship while in the U.S.M.C.

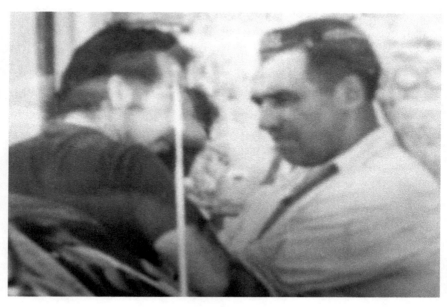

(2) Sedillo and Trafficker

(3) Ten kilos of Heroin seized in Guadalajara, Mexico

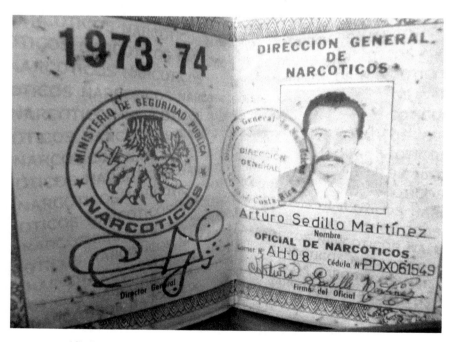

(4) Costa Rica makes Sedillo a member of its Narcotics Unit

**MA COUNTRY ATTACHE ART SEDILLO (RED
LT. JORGE "LENO" LATINEZ AT CRASH SITE
AT A BANANA FINCA OUTSIDE DAVID, PANAMA**

(5) With Lino and others during $2,000,000 cocaine seizure

9 781478 797470